JAPAN
IN 60 EASY STEPS

For everyone in search of adventure in Japan

Axel Schwab

JAPAN
IN 60 EASY STEPS

The compact and comprehensive travel guide with expert tips

Munich & Tokyo

2024

© 2018-2024 Axel Schwab, Munich, Germany.
All rights reserved.

Illustration and text: **Axel Schwab**
Cover design: **Simon Marchner**
Translator: **Jane Riester**
Proof Reading: **Alana Campbell**

2nd edition, revised June 2024

Independently published
Contact: Axel Schwab, Thierschstr. 37, D-80538 Munich
           japan@axelschwab.com

ISBN: 979-8-5408-9033-5

Table of Contents

Preface 8

Maiko Level 9
   Deciding when to go .... 季節 10
   Booking your trip .... 予約 12
   Ordering a JR Pass .... ジャパンレールパス 14
   Using maps in Japan .... 地図 16
   Preparing your smartphone .... アプリ 18
   Internet access on the go .... モバイル 20
   What to pack .... 荷物 22
   Buying presents .... おみやげ 24
   Adieu to tickets .... 切符 26
   Getting in the mood for Japan ... 日本 28

Sumo Level 29
   Breakfast on a shoestring .... 朝食 30
   Using chopsticks .... 箸 32
   Eating sushi correctly .... 寿司 34
   Enjoying tonkatsu .... 豚カツ 36
   Slurping noodles loudly .... 麺 38
   Conveyor-belt sushi .... 回転寿司 40
   Visiting cat cafés .... 猫カフェ 42
   Trying wagashi .... 和菓子 44
   Staying at a ryokan .... 旅館 46
   Saving money with teishoku .... 定食 48

Geisha Level 49
- Taking the subway .... 地下鉄 50
- Reading maps / Finding addresses .. 住所 52
- Using air conditioners .... エアコン 54
- Getting to know konbinis .... コンビニ 56
- Disposing of waste .... ごみ 58
- To smoke or not to smoke? .... 喫煙/禁煙 60
- Appreciating service .... サービス 62
- Taking a taxi .... タクシー 64
- Using the toilet correctly .... トイレ 66
- Changing shoes .... 靴 68

Samurai Level 69
- Collecting stamps .... 御朱印所 70
- Booking cars and driving .... 車 72
- Conforming to etiquette .... 気配り 74
- Rules for photographers .... 写真 76
- Bathing at a sentō .... 銭湯 78
- Understanding gestures .... 仕草 80
- Opening doors .... ドア 82
- Taking the bus .... バス 84
- Forwarding suitcases .... 宅急便 86
- Feasting on the train .... 弁当 88

Ninja Level 89
Renting a karaoke box .... カラオケボックス ... 90
Singing karaoke .... カラオケ 92
Budget feasting .... 食べ物 94
Shopping for souvenirs .... おみやげ 96
100 yen shops 100円ショップ 98
50 shades of thanks .... ありがとう 100
Doing your washing .... 洗濯物 102
At the launderette .... コインランドリー .. 104
Printing in konbinis .... ネットプリント 106
Buying canned coffee .... 缶コーヒー 108

Shogun Level 109
Shrines and temples .... 神社/お寺 110
Getting drunk in an izakaya .... 居酒屋 112
Surviving the forces of nature ...... 地震/台風 114
Beating the rain .... 雨 116
Wrapping presents .... 風呂敷 118
Going to a love hotel .... ラブホテル 120
Finding yourself .... 座禅/武道/茶道 .. 122
Searching for ikigai .... 生き甲斐 124
Internalising Ichi-go Ichi-e .... 一期一会 126
Ordering a personal seal .... 判子 128

Index 129
Notes 132

Preface

I first visited Japan 30 years ago, initially to study, and later worked as an engineer for 5 years in Tokyo. Since the very beginning I have been totally fascinated by the country and travel there every year - as long as no pandemic prevents me from doing so. I would like to share my experiences with you in this book and help you to have a perfect trip. It doesn't matter if you've never been to Japan before, or if you are planning a return visit. There is something for everybody.

You don't need to learn the language or be familiar with every particularity of Japanese culture to do the activities in this book. Every now and then I have inserted Japanese characters to make it easier for you to navigate everyday Japanese life. I have divided the information in the book into 60 steps and 6 levels which get harder as you progress. The final two levels are aimed at encouraging you to try out a few things you may not have attempted without this guide. I'll show you, for example, how to use a karaoke machine, visit a love hotel or how to order your own personal seal.

Throughout, I focus on information which is relevant to your trip and which will save you money. Things that you would find in any standard travel guide or that you could quickly discover for yourself, have been left out.

Short links save you the effort of typing in long web addresses and provide up-to-date information on the currently valid entry requirements. Please refer to the notes at the end of the book. Have fun planning your trip and enjoy your stay in Japan!

Axel Schwab, June 2024

Maiko Level

Like a **Maiko** (舞妓) at the start of her training to become a geisha, you are poised to take the first step on your trip to Japan. A good plan and thorough preparation are important if you want to happily immerse yourself in Japanese life.

Deciding when to go   季節

All travel plans begin with the question of when to travel. If you're flying to Japan for the first time, you'll open your travel guide and read, "Spring and autumn are the best time to visit Japan." Having lived there for five years, I can reveal that Japan is a beautiful destination in all seasons; it just depends on what you would like to do. Personally, I avoid the period from June to September. It often rains in **June;** I find **July** and **August** too hot; and in **September,** too, there are frequent typhoons with heavy rainfall. If you want to climb Mount Fuji, however, or savour the atmosphere of a summer festival with a magnificent firework display, or if you can only travel during the summer holidays, then don't let yourself be put off. My personal aversion to the Japanese **summer** dates back to the days when I had to go to the office in a suit and tie. At temperatures of over 30°C and humidity levels of 90%, the contrast between outdoors and the air-conditioned offices is not my idea of fun.

If you want to experience the legendary **cherry blossom season** during your first visit, you should travel to Japan in the **spring.** Bear in mind, though, that many travel during this time (the Japanese school holidays are from late March to early April). Prices for hotels and flights are a little higher than usual, and you should book in October or November of the previous year at the latest. But when exactly is the best time to experience the cherry blossom in Japan? As temperatures rise, the trees come into bloom gradually from South to North. Guided by a TV reporter, the nature-loving Japanese can follow the progress of the cherry blossom live on the evening news. When I go over for the cherry blossom season, to Tokyo for example, I fly in mid- to late March and stay for at least four weeks until around mid-April. That way I'm guaranteed to experience the cherry blossom throughout its

entire cycle, from when the first buds open, while the flowers are in full bloom, and until the blossoms wither and fall. This lasts about two weeks, but the start varies considerably depending on the weather. Now, not everyone has that much holiday or can only travel during the Easter holidays. In 2023, the cherry blossom in Tokyo already started on 14th March, while in 2024 it began on 29th March. In 2023, I was still able to enjoy the full blossom near Mount Fuji on 4th April. If you arrive too late, you have to be flexible and travel further north or to the mountains. But even in Tokyo, you can still enjoy the blossoms of the later cherry tree species in some parks.

When the **leaves change colour** and temperatures are mild, the **autumn** is an attractive time to visit. Don't forget, though, that this colourful spectacle reaches its high point in Tokyo beginning of December. The further into the cooler, more mountainous regions you go, the earlier this is. I have experienced delightfully colourful woodlands in Iwate Prefecture in mid-October, yet taken some great photos in Nikko at the end of the month.

The **wintertime** has its own special charm, and I particularly enjoy the quiet period around New Year. In Tokyo, the days are often clear and sunny, allowing a glimpse of the snow-capped Fuji-san which at other times is shrouded in cloud and mist. Bear in mind that many museums and shops are closed between 28th Dec. and 3rd January. Shinto shrines are busy over New Year.
www.gomap.de/**dwtg**

#Tip: The peak travel season for the Japanese is during **Golden Week** (29th April – 6th May), **Obon** in mid-August and the **New Year** (28th December – 6th January). Try to avoid travelling around Japan at these times, if you can.

Booking your trip   予約

You've decided when to travel; now the question is: package or customised tour? That depends on your personal preferences. If you are visiting Japan for the first time and don't want to have to take care of every detail, then a tour organised by a travel company offers several advantages. Are you generally not a fan of group travel and would like to plan your trip to suit your wishes or just be flexible when you get there? Then you should book everything yourself or get your travel agent or tour company to organise your personalised holiday for you. I always take care of everything myself and can therefore give you some tips on **booking hotels and flights.** We'll look at the subject of the Japan Rail Pass and car rental later on.

Many people already have a preferred portal which guarantees them best prices when booking a hotel. Unfortunately, many Japanese hotels are not covered at all by these portals or only a limited number of tariffs are offered. In the case of a hotel in Miyajima, my usual portal only offered me half board at a price of ¥25,000; a different, international one, on the other hand, also gave me the option of an overnight stay including breakfast for ¥10,000. In the end, I booked the same room, including breakfast, for only ¥8100 via **Agoda.**

This online booking platform is popular with Asian travellers and therefore has a wider range of hotels in Japan. The company is based in Singapore, but belongs to an American tour operator which also owns Booking.com, Kayak and OpenTable. So where's the catch? How can it be that a hotel room is offered almost 20% cheaper?

The cancellation conditions are the same, but the difference lies in the payment procedure. In the case of the cheaper offers, you don't pay at the hotel. Instead you pay Agoda by credit card five days in advance. This has always worked well for me, with the exception of a hotel in Niigata some years ago. Agoda, however, was not to blame here, but rather my bank which blocked all credit cards due to a data leak and sent my new card to my home address. Not very helpful, considering I was in Japan. As I was unable to provide a valid credit card number within 24 hours, Agoda cancelled the reservation. If you want to be on the safe side, you can authorise immediate payment when you book. This can even be an advantage if your currency is stronger against the yen at the time of booking than during your trip. It's a good idea to print out the PDF booking confirmation right away.
www.gomap.de/**bokn**

#Tip: I recommend you **book your flight** at least three to four months before your trip. If you are flexible enough to fly any day of the week, you may even find a convenient direct flight and so avoid the hassle of airport stopovers/connecting flights. In my experience, these flights are usually always fully booked, so don't wait around hoping to snap up a last-minute bargain. You can read about **driving licences** and **car rental** from page 72. From page 86 onwards, there's everything you need to know about **transporting luggage** and information about **transfers to and from the airport.**

Ordering a JR Pass   ジャパンレールパス

Before every visit to Japan you should ask yourself, is it worth getting a **Japan Rail Pass** (ジャパンレールパス) or not? After the price increase of almost 70% in October 2023, the purchase of the 7-day pass is only worthwhile for at least three longer journeys on the Shinkansen in combination with short journeys. A Japan Rail Pass has never been worthwhile if you are staying within Tokyo, Osaka or another big city and only plan one or two short excursions in the immediate vicinity. If you plan to travel long distances by express train a few times, the Japan Rail Pass is often still worthwhile.

The Japan Rail Pass is valid for 7, 14 or 21 days and can be used on almost all JR trains in Japan. The only exceptions are the **Shinkansen express trains** *Nozomi* and *Mizuho*, which you have been able to use since November 2023, but have to pay a distance-based surcharge for each journey. A *Hikari* from Tokyo to Kyoto takes only 20-30 minutes longer than a *Nozomi*, which is why the necessary surcharge of ¥4960 is hardly worthwhile when using the Rail Pass. Those travelling to Japan for the first time often take the classic route from Tokyo to Kyoto, Nara and Himeji to Hiroshima. On the way back, you make a stopover in Osaka. This journey is definitely cheaper with the Japan Rail Pass for 7 days than with individual tickets.

Travelling in normal class is already more comfortable than in 1st class in many other countries, but if you want to treat yourself to something special, I can highly recommend the Japan Rail Pass 1st class **"Green Car"**. There is even an additional service for food and drinks at your seat, while the snack trolleys in normal class were abolished in 2023.

You can buy a **voucher** for the **Japan Rail Pass** outside Japan. This is only valid for three months, so don't buy yours too early. (If you cancel your trip, it is possible to receive a refund minus 15% cancellation fee.) The voucher can then be exchanged in Japan at a dedicated **"Japan Rail Pass Exchange Office"** upon presentation of your passport and tourist visa. The offices are to be found at airports and major railway stations. Here, you can also indicate from when the pass should be valid for and make any **seat reservations** for trips you have planned with the Shinkansen (no reservations at the airport).

It is now possible to buy the Japan Rail Pass directly on the Japan Railways website at no extra charge. Only if you buy the Rail Pass directly can you make your **seat reservations online** up to one month before your journey. Otherwise, seat reservations must be made at a ticket machine or directly at the service counter.

If you only want to explore a certain part of Japan extensively by train, you should take a look at the various **regional passes** from **JR East** as an alternative to the Japan Rail Pass.

With a lot of time and little money, you can buy the **Seishun 18 Kippu** during the low season – it is only valid on local trains.
www.gomap.de/**jrps**

#Tip: If you want to know how much you can save with the JR Pass, use the **"Rail Pass Search"** from **Jorudan** to find out the prices of individual tickets. Unfortunately, their "Norikae Annai" app is currently only available in Apple's Japanese App Store.

With the **SmartEx app,** you can buy train tickets with reserved seats at a lower price on some routes; app only available in the US, Canada, Australia and Asia.

Using maps in Japan 地図

I used to advise any Japanese traveller who was about to venture into the urban jungle of Tokyo or Osaka for the first time not to attempt this without a detailed **map,** *chizu* (地図). Nowadays, when almost everyone has a smartphone in their pocket, it's enough to equip yourself with the right **map app** to guide you around your chosen destination.

If you have mobile internet access in Japan (for more tips, see p. 20), you can use either **Google Maps** or **Apple Maps,** depending on your personal preference and the device you use.

It is sometimes difficult to enter a Japanese address correctly but fortunately there is a simple method: use the telephone number of the destination address. Whether it's a restaurant, shop, museum or even public park, each can be found by means of its telephone number. In Japan itself this works extremely well with both Google and Apple Maps. A telephone number is unique and also easier to type in than a complicated Japanese address, which is why this feature has been the tried-and-tested method in Japanese navigation systems for decades. It also works with rental cars (p. 72) and usually with taxis (p. 64) for numbers listed in the phone book. So while it works well for businesses, it can be less effective for private addresses and things like Airbnb. If you'd like to try out this feature at home with Google Maps, bear in mind that it will only work if you change the language to Japanese and the destination address must lie within the map section. Enter, for example, "Japan" first of all and then the telephone number "+81 3-3433-5111" to find Tokyo Tower. If the extra cost of mobile internet access puts you off, you can download offline maps for the places you plan to visit.

Recently, this is even possible with Google Maps in Japan, but not all functions are available offline. A good alternative is the map app **MAPS.ME** which is based on data from **OpenStreetMap**. While still at home, planning freaks can use Google Maps to save all the sights they want to visit and routes they want to take in their own maps. These can be exported as KML files and then sent by e-mail to your smartphone and opened with the offline map app MAPS.ME. Before travelling you can get an excellent overview with the **Google Earth** software. Try this out with my map of the area around the Imperial Palace (Tour 5 in the *Tokyo Maze* book). The map link is www.gomap.de/**tkio.** Here you can click on the vertical three dots icon to access additional features and select "Export to KML/KMZ". Then start the download of the KMZ file with the blue selection button "Download". If you have Google Earth installed, all you have to do is double-click on the KMZ file and you can wander in 3D through the "urban canyons" around the main railway station and fly over the Imperial Palace. You can find these online maps for half of the 42 tours in my Tokyo walking guide. Save the KMZ files for the desired tours at home on your phone and access them on the spot via the bookmarks in MAPS.ME.

www.gomap.de/**maps**

#Tip: If you have mobile internet access in Japan (p. 20) I recommend you use **Google Maps** rather than **MAPS.ME** because of the superior presentation and readability.

Preparing your smartphone   アプリ

Alongside the maps app you will need some additional ones to help you find your way round in Japan. Of course, if you are permanently online, Google Maps works fine when using public transport and also includes information on departure times for most means of transport. However, I personally prefer other **apps,** *apuri* (アプリ), for planning journeys.

The best offline app for subways and trains is **City Rail Map,** featuring offline Metro maps and route planners for a large number of cities worldwide. The first city is free, so choose Kyoto, Osaka or Tokyo by way of introduction. Other cities can be activated for a fee, if required. If you have online access while travelling, you can download **Japan Travel** to your mobile phone. The free route planning functions are very extensive; there are also warnings of earthquakes and storms.

Holders of JR Passes can use the **Japan Transit Planner** by Jorudan, as it offers more features for planning train journeys (currently only web version). For example, you can specify whether you have a *Japan Rail Pass* or *Tokyo Subway Ticket* (p. 51), which is taken into account when calculating the fare. Because this only works with online access, you can plan the journeys with Wi-Fi in the hotel and save them with screenshots or send them to yourself as a text in an e-mail if you don't have internet access while travelling. If you plan your journeys on your computer, all platform and carriage numbers are given in the text. Sadly, this does not work for free on a mobile phone. I put the **Citymapper** app through its paces in Tokyo, but most of the suggested routes were poor, and it did not offer details of departure times.

Of the many **restaurant finder apps** on offer, I use only the Japanese market leader, **GuruNavi** - and then only occasionally. Bear in mind, however, that GuruNavi, like many other restaurant search and rating apps, is financed almost exclusively through advertising supplied by the featured eateries. Consequently, the more these pay, the better placed they are. A more independent alternative, with numerous customer ratings and photos, is **Tabelog's** Japanese website. Sadly, there is only a Japanese app. Tabelog's English restaurant search shows far fewer restaurants.

Imiwa is a good, free dictionary for use on iPhones. It lets you look up Japanese words quickly when you're on the move and are searching round for a translation. The app takes up just under 1 GB of storage space, but also works offline. Android users can use **Aedict.** For translating in the other direction, for example to get an idea of what's written on a sign or menu, you can use **Google Translate.** It is now possible to get a simultaneous translation of a camera image from **Japanese** to **English,** even offline. Google can't cope with handwritten menus and some complex Japanese characters, but the **Yomiwa** app can help here – subject to a charge. With any luck, though, you will be able to recognise some familiar terms on an otherwise completely indecipherable menu. The **VoiceTra** app recognises a number of languages. Just speak into the microphone and the translation is displayed and read aloud.

www.gomap.de/**apps**

#Tip: Don't forget to take the appropriate **travel adapter** for use with your chargers and computer. Japan has type A plugs and **sockets,** whereas in many parts of Europe, Asia and Australia, type C is widespread. American visitors with devices using type B plugs (3 pins) should get an adapter to be on the safe side, since most sockets in Japan only take 2-pin plugs.

www.gomap.de/**trad**

Internet access on the go　　　　モバイル

There are six different ways of accessing the internet with your mobile phone – and I have tested them all locally.
International roaming may be the most convenient way of doing this, but it is also the most expensive.
When moving around in Tokyo I used to rely on **free wi-fi** in cafés and railway stations. Starbucks, for example, has a dense network of outlets, and once you've registered you can use the wi-fi network in all of them. You'll find a precise description on Starbucks' Japanese website. As you need to be online to do this, I recommend you register from home or, at the latest, when you arrive in your hotel in Japan.
Apart from crowded train and metro stations, you can find free wi-fi service in most **Lawson** shops (p. 56). You can use it via NTT Docomo's **d Wi-Fi service,** which requires the **d POINT CLUB app.**
Of course, almost all cafés and restaurants offer free wi-fi nowadays; just ask the staff: *"Wi-fi arimasu ka?"* and they're sure to be of assistance. The **Japan Wi-Fi auto-connect** app is very useful, as it does the job of registering at wi-fi hotspots in 24-hour stores (p. 56), stations and other locations for you. The obvious disadvantage of free wi-fi is, whenever you need it most, it doesn't work or is so slow that you miss your train.
Between 2013 and 2015 I used a **rental SIM card** from Softbank. You can order it via the internet and collect the SIM card at the Softbank counter at the airport. You are charged a small fee per day and a one-off administration charge.

If you then use the internet, you face relatively high charges per day. This can get very expensive in the long term, and for this reason I only activate data use via my phone in an emergency and otherwise use free wi-fi hotspots, where available. A big advantage of such rental SIM cards is that phone calls are naturally much cheaper and you don't pay expensive roaming charges on calls from home.

A less expensive way of accessing the internet is with a **prepaid SIM card,** though these should only be used for surfing and not to phone with. This naturally only works if your phone has no SIM lock. You'll find a wide range of such prepaid data SIMs in Japan itself. In 2019, I bought a "Visitor SIM" from B-mobile at Haneda Airport and paid only ¥2970 for 7 GB to be used within 21 days. An **eSIM** is more practical because you can still receive calls with your internal SIM. I have tested the **Airalo app** extensively in May 2024 and can recommend it without restrictions. www.gomap.de/**inac**

#Tip: If you're travelling in a group, a **mobile wi-fi router** is the perfect solution. You receive a **"Pocket wi-fi"** device the size of a cigarette packet. This dials into the mobile network and creates a wi-fi hotspot. All devices can then connect to it. There are a number of providers of wi-fi routers on the internet; you'll find recommended ones via the above link. The simplest way is to have the device sent directly to the first hotel. Then you just put it in the return envelope provided and throw it in the letterbox at the airport before your return flight.

What to pack   荷物

Long before I travel anywhere I compile a list of things to pack using Excel, though you can use any other **spreadsheet program.** The advantage of a such a list is that you're not caught out on the day before you leave when you notice that your suitcase is far too heavy or that you might also need a **light waterproof jacket** or more **shoes.** If you still have a little to spare before you reach the maximum weight allowance, you could buy a few presents (p. 24).

For a two-week trip, there's no need to plan on **washing** any clothes. However, if you're staying for three to four weeks, it's definitely worth considering when and where you can do some washing during the course of your trip (p. 102). You don't need to include too many items on your list.

My list consists of the following categories: Quantity, designation, individual weight and total weight. Don't forget to weigh your suitcase when it's empty and enter this on your list. Besides the one for my main suitcase, I also make a list for my hand luggage. If I need to, I can then swap items between check-in and carry-on baggage until the weights add up.

Remember to include these important items on your list for Japan: In winter, warm **woolly socks** are especially nice to have if you are staying in a traditional inn, a *ryokan* (p. 46) or if you want to visit any temples. Make sure your socks don't have holes in them, as you will have to take your shoes off at the entrance. **Shoes** which are easy to slip on and off are a real advantage here. If you are travelling in the period between June and September, you should definitely have a good-quality, breathable **waterproof jacket** with a hood on your list.

Particularly when you are outside during a typhoon, an umbrella is of no help in keeping you dry. As a rule, the high humidity in summer means that functional textiles are preferable to pure cotton ones. Incidentally, Tokyo lies at the same latitude as the Mediterranean island of Malta. So don't forget sun cream on your city trip, as it's easy to get a sunburnt face if you are out all day, even in spring and autumn. I recommend you keep your head covered in summer.

Payment in **cash** is still widespread in Japan; credit cards are not accepted everywhere. It makes sense, therefore, to have some cash with you for the first few days. The limit for the amount of money you can take into the country is 1 million yen, so that's not a problem. The exchange rates for withdrawing cash from ATMs are better than withdrawing yen in your home country or exchanging cash in Japan. So if you want to save money, you should use your credit card to withdraw cash from the ATM as soon as you arrive. **Important:** Never let the ATM debit in your home currency, but always in yen! In Japan you can get cash from the **ATMs** at the **post office** or **7-Eleven** stores (p. 56). The additional fees of ¥110 or ¥220 from ¥20,000 are reasonable.

#Tip: I used to often get a cold on long flights thanks to the dry air inside the plane. Since I started using a sea water **nasal spray** this is no longer a problem. If you tend to be troubled by dry eyes, on the other hand, include some **eye drops** in your hand luggage. You can recognise the true Japan experts on the plane, by the way. They're the ones who slip off their shoes after take-off and put on the **thick socks** or **slippers** they've brought with them.

Buying presents　　　　　　　おみやげ

The giving of **small gifts, *omiyage*** (おみやげ), is a widespread cultural tradition in Japan and one which I have always adhered to since my first visit to Japan. When they return from a trip – even inside Japan – the Japanese usually bring back a regional speciality as a gift for their families, friends and colleagues. In offices in Japan there are always delicious biscuits, small cakes or **salty rice crackers, *osenbei*** (煎餅), to go with the coffee. For many Japanese, this social obligation is also something of a burden and they often buy something to have in reserve in case they get home and realise they've forgotten someone.

When I fly to Japan nowadays I always take a few small gifts with me. If you don't know anyone in Japan and are not meeting a business partner, it is not absolutely necessary to take gifts with you. But if you do have 1-2 kg of your baggage allowance to spare, I suggest you take some confectionery with you. It's a particularly good idea if you are planning to spend a longer period at a small, family-run hotel or ryokan or if you do get to know someone. You'll be prepared for all eventualities. As a tourist, you won't be expected to return the compliment if you are given a small gift at some point. On the other hand, if your gut feeling tells you that someone has made a real effort on your behalf, or the service you have received was exceptional and went beyond what you had expected, then you can express your thanks in this way as tipping is not customary in Japan (exception, p. 65). What makes a suitable gift? If you're travelling in the autumn or winter, you might like to take some traditional Christmas biscuits or other edible specialities from your home country. Avoid taking anything which is coated in chocolate in August and September for obvious reasons.

Tea is another good choice (something unusual, but under no circumstances green tea). Foreign brand sweets and confectionery also go down well. It's best to buy things which you like yourself. If there's anything left over at the end of your trip, you can eat it yourself and so make room for the souvenirs you've bought in Japan for your loved ones.

If you do notice when in Japan that you need a small present or if you get a sudden craving for your favourite **chocolate bar,** you could pop into one of the many convenience stores, e.g. **Family-Mart** (p. 56). The one on the ground floor of the Ebisu Garden Place in Tokyo stocks a number of foreign products.

Another place to buy sweets brands from abroad is in shops of the **Don Quijote** chain (p. 98).

www.gomap.de/**gsck**

#Tip: Here's a real insider tip for avoiding going over your baggage allowance and still maximising your haul of Japanese souvenirs. When travelling through Japan, I always try to buy gifts totalling the exact weight of the presents I brought with me originally. I also try to only buy things which are really light, such as tea or rice crackers.

Before you leave, you can stock up on heavier things like **Matcha Kitkat, sweet rice cakes** *mochi* (餅)**, sake** *nihonshu* (日本酒) and **Japanese whisky** or **gin** (Craft Gin Kanomori by Yomeishu is my favourite) the duty-free area you'll find at every airport and take these on board as additional hand luggage.0 I even once bought a 220-V rice cooker.

Adieu to tickets   切符

Thankfully, the times when you needed to buy a **ticket,** *kippu* (切符), at the ticket machine for every subway ride are over. Even if you are only in Japan for a short time, it pays to buy a prepaid card. You simply touch the reader provided at the barriers with the smart card. It basically doesn't matter which of the cards you buy, as they are all recognised by the various transport providers in that area. **Suica** (JR East in Tokyo, Niigata and Sendai), **PASMO** (subway in Tokyo), **ICOCA** (JR West in Osaka, Kyoto and Kobe), **TOICA** (JR Central in Nagoya), **manaca** (subway in Nagoya), **PiTaPa** (Kansai), **Kitaca** (JR Hokkaidō), **SUGOCA** (JR Kyūshū), **nimoca** (Nishitetsu), **Hayakaken** (subway in Fukuoka). Before you use public transport for the first time, buy the card on offer. To do this, you will need cash. As soon as the amount on the card is used up, you can top it up again at any of the machines provided.

By the way, the cards (except PiTaPa) not only work on public transport, but also in station shops, newer vending machines and many of the 24-hour stores (p. 56).

If you lose your card, the money is also lost – in the same way as if it were cash. To avoid this happening, it is also possible to have yourself issued with a personalised card printed with your name. You can have such cards replaced and receive the outstanding amount at the time the card was blocked. In a fundamentally honest country like Japan it is highly unlikely that the thief would use up the balance immediately.

#Note: The last time I tried, it was not possible to get a personalised PASMO from the new machines with the large display. At the older ones with the smaller display it worked perfectly. Select "Purchase PASMO" and "Personal user PASMO". First you have to agree to the use of your personal data, then you select "Adult".

Children's cards can only be purchased from sales personnel at the ticket office. A maximum of 15 characters may be used to enter your name, so abbreviate it if necessary. Next, you have to indicate your gender and date of birth and enter a telephone number. If you do not have a Japanese telephone number, you can simply use your own number including the area code but without the country code. Finally, you agree to the privacy policy and your personalised PASMO is issued.

If you only visit Japan once for a maximum of 28 days, you can buy a **Welcome Suica** or **PASMO PASSPORT** at the airport and major railway stations. Due to delivery problems, neither these nor normal Suica/PASMO are currently available. If you are using an iPhone, proceed as described in the tip below.

iPhone users can transfer their physical Suica or PASMO card to their **Apple Wallet** and set it to Express Mode for payments in public transport. This then works automatically without Face ID, Touch ID or passcode. It is particularly practical to use on the **Apple Watch,** as you don't have to take your phone out of your pocket at the barriers. The Suica or PASMO cards in the Apple Wallet can still be topped up with cash, but only at a few ticket machines and in 24-hour stores. It is easier to charge them directly with **Apple Pay.** In my tests in April 2024, this only worked with Mastercard and Amex, but not with Visa!
www.gomap.de/**epay**

#Tip: If you own an **iPhone,** already use **Apple Pay** and do not have a Suica or PASMO card, then you do not need to buy a prepaid card locally. You can create one right in **Apple Wallet** before you travel and top it up with a minimum amount of ¥1000. You can find the instructions for this via the short link printed above.

Getting in the mood for Japan 日本

So, your trip to **Japan, *Nippon*** (日本), is planned, flights and hotels booked. You're beginning to get excited even though your holiday is still many weeks off. Why not whet your appetite for Japanese culture right now? If you live in or close to a big city, it's relatively easy. You're sure to find a good selection of excellent, authentic restaurants, cafés and attractive Japanese shops. Put **Japanese hospitality, *omotenashi*,** to the test and book a table at a Japanese restaurant or go shopping in a Japanese store. While you're there, mention your planned holiday in Japan and, with any luck, you'll be given a few good tips from the Japanese staff.

#Tip: Another good way of preparing for your trip to Japan is to watch TV documentaries and reports. The best option here is **NHK World-JAPAN** via its website or its apps for Android and Apple. These let you follow live broadcasts in English and watch other exciting, informative material. For Japan novices, I recommend NHK World's video-on-demand series "Easy Travel Japanese". I enjoy watching their well-researched travel documentaries using Apple TV. In Japan activate the **push notifications** in the app to receive warnings about **earthquakes** and **tsunamis** (p. 114).
www.gomap.de/**nhkw**

#Tip: If you are dependent on a **wheelchair** for your trip, you will find a lot of helpful information on the **Accessible Japan** website. In particular, hotels that are wheelchair accessible, detailed accessibility reviews for many tourist attractions and information on how to get around on public transport with disabilities.
www.accessible-japan.com

Sumo Level

Besides training, eating is very important for **Sumo wrestlers** (力士). Japanese cuisine, *washoku* (和食), even has UNESCO World Heritage status. Take every possible opportunity to savour this refined art of cooking in all its variety.

Breakfast on a shoestring 朝食

I start the day with a good breakfast, but my first ever Japanese **breakfast,** *chōshoku* (朝食), was not at all to my taste. Back in 1993, before I was able to move into my student accommodation, I was lodged in a business hotel for one night where I was served **rice, grilled fish,** a bowl of **miso soup** (a traditional Japanese soup made of fish stock and **soy bean paste,** *miso* (味噌), often with tofu and seaweed) and **pickled radish** for breakfast. Although I have come to love Japanese food in the meantime, in those days rice and fish were not my idea of breakfast and I went out that very day and bought myself cornflakes and milk.

Now when I visit a **traditional inn,** *ryokan* (旅館), I have got used to Japanese breakfast, though in hotels I still go for the **"Continental Breakfast"** option. Breakfast is often not included in hotel room prices and at ¥2000-4000 is rather expensive. If you only choose the tasteless toast with a little jam and butter, you're not really getting good value for money. I've therefore put together a few ideas for getting the day off to a good start:

Most rooms have a **kettle** to boil water with, and the free supply of tea and instant coffee is regularly refilled when you've used it up. If you're in a hurry one particular morning, you could buy something for breakfast the night before from a **24-hour store.** Cakes, pastries, yoghurt, orange juice, or whatever else you enjoy eating in the morning. If you're a fan of filter coffee, you can also get this to make yourself – vacuum-packed, it comes complete with filter and cardboard filter holder. If it has to be **freshly-ground coffee,** and you have a little time to spare, you could even have breakfast at the 24-hour store itself as many have somewhere to sit.

A good and generally cheaper alternative to breakfast at **Starbucks Coffee** (there are over 1000 branches in Japan) is to be had at café chains with names like **Beck's Coffee Shop, Café de Crié, Caffe Veloce, Doutor, Excelsior Caffé, Ginza Renoir, Hoshino Coffee, Moriva Coffee, Pronto, St. Marc Café, Tully's Coffee, Ueshima Coffee** and **Vie de France**. Watch out for their breakfast specials, normally referred to as the **"Morning Set"**. There's toast or a sandwich with a beverage and occasionally also an egg. Prices for a "Morning Set" are often as little as around ¥500. All the 24-7 burger chains and family restaurants (e.g. **Royal Host**) offer a "Morning Set" to entice customers in for breakfast. Even if you choose from a selection of pastries at the self-service counter and order a coffee to go with it, you rarely have to pay more than ¥1000. Here is a list of websites of all the cafés mentioned above: www.gomap.de/**cafe**

#Tip: You can save on your afternoon coffee or tea break with a **"Cake Set"**, but the choice of drinks is limited to **"Blend Coffee"** or **"Blend Tea"**. Many cafés also offer reasonably priced **sandwiches, pasta** or even **pizza,** if you don't fancy eating Japanese at lunchtime or in the evening for a change.

#Tip: Anyone who discovers *nattō* (納豆) made from fermented whole soy beans at the breakfast buffet should try it at least once. As with mould cheese, humanity can be divided into two parts: Either you love the sticky, slimy texture with its strong smell or you hate it.

Using chopsticks   箸

Presumably you'll be able to have breakfast without using **chopsticks,** *hashi* (箸), but sooner or later you'll have to get to grips with them. If you haven't already practised using them at home, here's a brief description of how to do it properly:

Hold one chopstick firmly between the base of the thumb and the ring finger and the other like a pencil, using only the tips of thumb and forefinger:

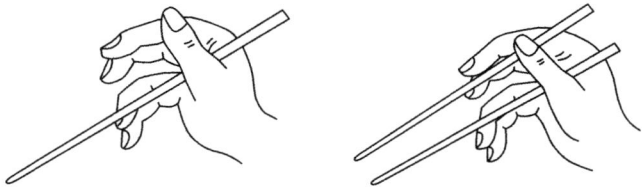

Use the fingers to move the upper chopstick and pick up the food with the tips of both chopsticks ("V" position).

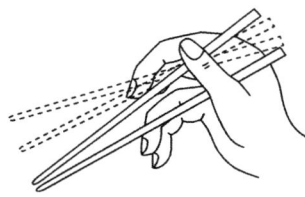

To help you avoid committing a faux pas right at the start of your trip to Japan, on the next page I'll show you the most important rules regarding the use of chopsticks.

Food should never be passed from one set of chopsticks to another but always put down on a plate or into a small bowl first. The only time chopsticks are used in this way is during a traditional funeral ceremony when relatives of the deceased together pick the bones from the ashes after cremation of the body and place them in the urn. It would be similarly shocking to stick your chopsticks upright in a bowl of rice, as this is the way rice is symbolically served to the dead.

As long as you are still eating, you should lay your chopsticks, for example between mouthfuls, on a **chopstick rest, *hashioki*** (箸置き), if provided. If you lay the chopsticks parallel across the bowl containing the soy sauce or the bowl of rice or miso soup, you are indicating that you have finished eating. If you are sharing a platter with several people, use the unused ends of the chopsticks to transfer the food onto your own plate.

Chopsticks are not intended to be used for skewering pieces of food. Nor should you use them to move plates and bowls around. Pointing at people with your chopsticks is also frowned upon. It is a bad habit to rub the chopsticks together to remove wood splinters. You should also avoid laying down chopsticks so that they cross.

#Tip: In cheaper restaurants there are often no chopstick rests. In this case, lay them on the paper sleeve or on your plate. Some Japanese simply fold the paper sleeve three times and bend this in such a way as to form a kind of rack. It is then possible to rest the chopsticks on the edge so they don't touch the table.

Eating sushi correctly 寿司 (すし)

If mastering the art of eating with chopsticks proves tricky, let me put your mind at rest right from the start: it really is OK to eat **sushi** (寿司) with your fingers. Here, too, there are a number of potential pitfalls, so I'd like to explain some of the key rules.
Use only a little **soy sauce, *shōyu*** (醤油). Ideally you should only help yourself to enough to cover the bottom of the bowl provided. When eating the finger-shaped *nigiri-zushi* (握り寿司), dip the fish side briefly until around a third of the fish is lightly coated in sauce. **Pickled ginger, *gari*** (ガリ), is never eaten at the same time as sushi, but always between the various types of fish, so that it neutralises the flavour of each in the mouth. On my last visit to a sushi restaurant in Berlin, I was forced to witness one diner positively drowning his sushi. He placed it, rice side down, in the centre of a bowl brimming with soy sauce and waited until the rice was well and truly marinated! To crown it all, he took a piece of ginger which he draped over each portion of sushi before popping it into his mouth! It's a mystery to me how anyone can enjoy such over-salted sushi.
Another bad habit consists of stirring **Japanese horseradish, *wasabi*** (山葵), into the soy sauce. This prevents its aromas developing properly. In Japan you will always find the correct amount of wasabi between fish and rice. If you don't like it, however, you can always say so. At a **conveyor-belt sushi** restaurant (p. 40) you can indicate whether you like wasabi or not, when you order. Wasabi is always served with **bite-sized portions of raw fish,** *sashimi* (刺身), and so-called **scattered sushi, *chirashi*** (ちらし).

Here you pick up as much or as little as you prefer with your chopsticks and place it on top of the fish which you then dip in the soy sauce. This all combines to create a perfect taste sensation in the mouth. If you are not given a wet towel, *oshibori,* at the restaurant it may be more pleasant to use chopsticks to eat your sushi. With nigiri sushi you should always take hold of the pieces lengthways because it is then less likely that they will fall apart. It takes a little practice, though, to dip the fish into the soy sauce correctly. It's easiest if you turn the sushi carefully on its side using your chopsticks and then fix the fish side and rice base between both. Now you can correctly dip just the fish side into the soy sauce. With **sushi rolls,** *maki* (巻き), you dip only one edge briefly into the soy sauce, otherwise it absorbs too much. An elegant way of eating so-called **battleship sushi,** *gunkan-maki* (軍艦巻き), is to spread a little soy sauce over the fish roe using a piece of pickled ginger. With the exception of the cone-shaped **rolls,** *temaki* (手巻き), sushi is always eaten whole, i.e. you do not bite pieces in half and you don't split them using your chopsticks. You should also never take the sushi apart by lifting the fish topping off the rice, as this constitutes an insult to the sushi chef. By the way, don't leave the sushi lying around too long, but eat it immediately after it is served.

#Tip: If you would like to find out more about sushi, there are several good books on the market:
www.gomap.de/**subk**

Enjoying tonkatsu 豚カツ (とんカツ)

Now that you have had some practice at using chopsticks, and given that eating only sushi could get boring after a while, I'd like to introduce you to another Japanese speciality. **Tonkatsu** (豚カツ) is not unlike a classic pork cutlet, but the Japanese have managed to take it to another level. The special breadcrumb coating, *panko,* makes them even crispier than a classic Wiener schnitzel. Depending on whether you prefer leaner or fattier meat, you can choose between pork fillet, *hire* (ヒレ), and a marbled cut, *rōsu* (ロース) at the tonkatsu restaurant. Personally, I prefer the juicier **rōsu-katsu.** Tonkatsu is always cut into strips and served with grated white cabbage and rice on the side, so that it can be eaten with chopsticks.

The first major hurdle to be overcome with tonkatsu is choosing the right sauce. A thick, brown sauce is poured over the meat. It usually comes from a large pot bearing the word **sauce** (ソース). Sometimes there are different sauces for different types of tonkatsu. If the restaurant staff don't show you which one you should take, it's best to ask. You can either pour a little sauce directly onto the meat or into the small bowl provided. If you are given such a bowl, there is often also a mill containing sesame seeds which you can mix with the sauce if you wish. I use a little **soy sauce,** *shōyu* (醤油), to season the white cabbage. In addition to the sauce, some people also traditionally like to add lemon and a little **salt,** *shio* (塩), to their meat. In many tonkatsu restaurants you'll find a tub of mustard, or a dollop is spooned onto the edge of your plate automatically.

Be careful, though. This is usually a very hot type of mustard which should be used sparingly on the meat or stirred into the sauce to taste. The quick lunchtime variation, **katsudon** (カツ丼), consists of meat on a bowlful of rice and garnished with a half-cooked egg.

If you should happen to visit **Nagoya** on your travels, be sure to try the local speciality, **miso-katsu.** The sauce contains miso and is usually poured more generously over the meat.

Another popular option in Japan is the variety with a **curry sauce.** For less than ¥1000 you can get pork cutlet curry at the ubiquitous chain **Curry House Coco Ichibanya.** If you prefer not to eat pork, perhaps for religious reasons, they also have variations with **beef** or **chicken.**

The **Maisen** restaurant is a Japanese institution and has a long tradition of serving tonkatsu, also using the excellent meat of the black *kurobuta* (黒豚) pig. The original restaurant is located in an old bathhouse within walking distance of the Omotesandō in Harajuku, Tokyo. At weekends there are often long queues, so I suggest you visit one of the many branches located all over Japan.
www.gomap.de/**tnkt**

#Tip: Have you decided to visit the original Maisen restaurant after all and are put off by the long queue? Then why not buy a katsu sandwich, **hirekatsu-sando,** or a **lunch box** to take away.

Slurping noodles loudly   麺

Japanese cuisine has a huge variety of **noodles,** *men* (麺), which can be classified into the following types: **rāmen** (ラーメン), **soba** (そば) and **udon** (うどん). While I favour a hot rāmen soup in winter, in the summer I prefer soba and udon which can also be dipped in delicious sauces and then slurped down indulgently. The noodles can also be eaten using chopsticks. Now that you've had some practice, you can hopefully use them to fish a bite-sized portion out of your bowl. You then suck them up into your mouth, making a loud slurping noise in the process – an essential part of eating noodles in Japan! Italian pasta, however, is not slurped but eaten in the conventional Western way with a fork.

Rāmen in particular is available in seemingly countless varieties, depending on the noodles, broth and topping used. The **noodles** are made of wheat flour, salt, water and sometimes eggs. They get their yellow colour from the addition of *kansui,* the name for the water of Lake Kan in Inner Mongolia where this type of noodle originated. Today, this ingredient is industrially produced. Food legislation prohibits its use in some countries like Germany, though imported noodles may contain it. Top-quality noodles are freshly prepared daily, but there are some which can be kept for a few days in the fridge, and the dried varieties keep for several months.

The **basic broth** consists of chicken or fish stock, *dashi* (出汁), or is made from boiled pig bones, *tonkotsu* (豚骨). Depending on the customer's wishes, either soy sauce, *shōyu* (醤油), soya bean paste, *miso* (味噌), or simply salt, *shio* (塩), is added during preparation.

As a **topping** you'll find spring onions, *negi* (葱), pork, *chāshū* (チャーシュー), vegetables, *yasai* (野菜), or hot meat sauce, *tantan* (担担). Freshly prepared **soba noodles** (手打ちそば), made of **buckwheat** are best enjoyed cold. They are served on a bamboo mat called a *zaru* (ざる) and are occasionally garnished with strips of seaweed, *nori* (海苔). Add a little wasabi, spring onion and possibly grated radish and spices to the accompanying sauce and dip the noodles in it. When you have finished eating you will be given a small jug containing *sobayu* (蕎麦湯), the thick water the noodles were cooked in. Pour this into the remaining sauce and enjoy it as a soup. If you do not receive any sobayu, you say: *"Sobayu o-negai shimasu"* – "Sobayu, please".

Now we come to the generally thicker **wheat noodles, udon.** The selection here is not as wide as with rāmen, but many restaurants also prepare them freshly every day. Soups with curry, *karē* (カレー), fried slices of tofu, *kitsune* (きつね), or battered and fried vegetables and shrimps, *tempura* (天ぷら) are popular choices.

www.gomap.de/**nudl**

#Tip: If you would like to savour unconventional udon from giant bowls in pleasant surroundings, I recommend the **TsuruTon-Tan** restaurant chain. You'll find a number of branches in **Tokyo** and **Osaka.** With any luck, you might get a window seat at the **Ginza Tōkyū Plaza** overlooking the Sukiyabashi junction.

Conveyor-belt sushi　　回転寿司

Outside Japan, I tend to avoid restaurants with **conveyor-belt sushi**, *kaiten-zushi* (回転寿司), apart from a few exceptions. In Japan, however, you can always enjoy fresh sushi without hesitation at such eateries, if you follow my advice. The classic conveyor belts, from which you pick up a small plate depending on what you fancy, are becoming rare or are supplemented by an additional "track" which delivers your individual sushi order fully automatically right under your nose.

If I'm very hungry, I also like to choose something from the belt, but many people are not aware that it is also possible to order directly at a conveyor-belt sushi restaurant. The advantage here is that you get fresh sushi which has not already done a few laps of the restaurant! It's easy to order. You write the appropriate number of each type of sushi you require on the small slips of paper found on the table which you then hand to the service staff. If necessary, they add the table number if you haven't already done so yourself.

Only if you would like to order several plates of the same dish, should you enter the quantity in a separate column, [皿数]. A plate of nigiri-sushi usually consists of two pieces anyway. A separate column is dedicated to *wasabi* [わさび]. If you don't like it, you can draw a circle around the word "without" [ぬき]. Sometimes you'll find the kanji character for "with", [入], which you should circle if you *do* want wasabi.

Nowadays most restaurants are equipped with tablets which make ordering even easier. Once you've placed your order, it doesn't take long for your sushi to be transported directly to your seat. Different restaurants have different ways of letting you know your sushi has arrived. Some make a sound as your dish arrives at your seat, some use different plates or have little signs, and in some restaurants the conveyor belt stops – in this case don't forget to press a button if necessary so the belt can move on!

Conveyor-belt sushi has a number of other extra features which newcomers should know about. You make your **tea** yourself by taking an empty cup and adding some matcha powder. Apparently, tourists have been known to scatter the powder over their sushi, thinking it was wasabi! Hot water is on tap at the counter. Be careful when pouring, as it is very hot. You can take **pickled ginger** from the tub yourself. I like to order a **miso soup** separately as well.

www.gomap.de/**ktsi**

#Tip: You can put together your sushi order as you please, picking dishes from the conveyor belt at any time, ordering via tablet or by consulting the menu and entering the numbers on the small slips of paper provided. Afterwards, the service staff count the empty plates and give you a printout of your order. You present this at the cash desk by the exit and pay.

Visiting cat cafés　　　　　　　猫カフェ

If you enjoy a good cup of coffee and like cats, then I have a disappointment in store for you: a **cat café,** *nekocafe* (猫カフェ), is first and foremost about cats. Coffee plays a subordinate role, for good reason. Although I have a cat-hair allergy, I have spared no effort in testing a few cat cafés.

Small apartments and long working hours may be the reasons why many Japanese do not have cats as pets and prefer to relax for a few hours in a cat café, playing with the cats, stroking them or simply taking pleasure in looking at them. Generally speaking, a **fee** for a visit to a cat café is based on the **amount of time spent** there, whereby the **minimum stay** is either 30 minutes or 1 hour. Normally, an hour costs roughly **¥1320,** however it's often more expensive on weekends than on weekdays.

Beverages are only available from vending machines. These are usually plain coffee and soft drinks in paper cups. If the price does not include drinks, you can pay a little extra and book the **"All you can drink"** option. So far, I've never come across cakes or other foods in a Japanese cat café, and it is not allowed to bring your own food. For this reason, the strict hygiene regulations relating to restaurants do not apply. They *do* apply, however, to cat cafés outside Japan which offer cakes and snacks. These can now be found in a number of Western cities. You can spend an agreeable time alone or with your family at a cat café, though in the latter case you can run up quite a bill as children usually pay the same price as adults. Some cat cafés have fixed feeding times in the morning and evening, which are a good opportunity to take photos or videos.

Please observe the following **rules** when visiting a cat café:
- Shoes and bags are to be left in a locker.
- Hands should be washed and disinfected beforehand.
- Any number of photos can be taken, but only without flash.
- Talking loudly is not permitted.
- Feeding is forbidden; some cafés sell treats.
- Cats must not be caught or carried around.
- Normal games and stroking are allowed.
- Sleeping cats must not be disturbed.

In addition to cat cafés there are also other animal cafés; **hedgehogs** and **owls** are right on trend at the moment because the young are so cute, *kawaii.* These are definitely not pets, but wild animals, which is why I would discourage you from visiting such cafés for reasons of animal welfare. What I have taken a look at has made me very sad. I remember a young owl, for example, which had a greasy mark on its head from being stroked too much.

#Tip: There are also huge differences between cat cafés when it comes to standards and facilities. In some, I had the feeling that the cats were considered purely as goods being marketed in desolate surroundings. The cats should have their own space to retreat to. I was impressed by the cafés operated by the **Cat Cafe Mocha** chain. There are currently nine of these in Tokyo and also branches in Kyoto, Nagoya, Osaka and other places.
www.gomap.de/**cats**

Trying wagashi 　　　　　　　　　　和菓子

You'll find a host of cafés in Japan, too, where you can enjoy a coffee and a piece of cake. But where the English might prefer tea and scones for their afternoon refreshment, Japan also boasts a highly developed tea-drinking culture! You don't necessarily have to book an elaborate tea ceremony. In many gardens and parks you can get a set for around ¥500 consisting of a cup of **matcha tea** and a piece of Japanese **confectionery** known as wagashi.

Wagashi (和菓子) are made of plant-based raw materials, usually sweet bean paste, *anko* (あんこ), sugar, agar-agar and occasionally pounded rice, *mochi* (餅). One variety of wagashi called **higashi** (干菓子) is drier and made out of pressed rice flour and sugar. The design and colour of these sweets varies according to the season.

Eat the wagashi before your tea, as their sweetness will help to tone down the bitterness of the matcha tea. With larger wagashi, take each sweet together with the *kaishi* paper underneath it onto the palm of your hand and cut it into bite-sized pieces using a *kuromoji,* the tiny wooden skewer provided. After you have eaten the wagashi, take the tea cup in both hands. Take this as an opportunity to practise for a formal tea ceremony and hold the side of the cup with your right hand, supporting it underneath with your left. Then turn the cup twice with your right hand so that the pretty front which was facing you before faces your host once more (i.e. turn it 180 degrees). You then drink the tea as you wish, in roughly three to four sips, turn the cup back again 180 degrees and put it down in front of you. That was just the simplified procedure for when each guest receives a tea cup. In a traditional tea ceremony, the cup is shared and participants drink one after the other.

At the beginning, therefore, before you take the cup in your hand you say "Osakini" which means something like "Excuse me for drinking before you". After taking a sip, the cup is often wiped with your right thumb and forefinger, then you wipe your fingers on the paper napkin provided. In some situations, you may also be given a cloth napkin, and this is used to wipe the area you drank from a second time. This wiping of the bowl is especially important if you have left a lipstick or chapstick mark on the cup. Before putting it down, admire the cup as a sign of appreciation towards the host.

There are many well established shops with a long tradition of selling wagashi. These shops are where the host of a private tea ceremony buys the appropriate sweets. The famous manufacturer, **Toraya** from Kyoto, has been in business since the 16th century and operates many branches throughout Japan.

www.gomap.de/**wgsi**

#Tip: If you want to buy fresh wagashi outside Japan, you'll discover that there are virtually none to be had. Take the opportunity while in Japan to take a course. In around two hours you'll get a basic insight into how to produce raw wagashi *(jō-namagashi)*. Once back from your holiday, you'll be able to use the main ingredients, where available, and make your own. Then you can surprise your visitors by putting on your own authentic tea ceremony.

If you are interested in short workshops on Japanese culture and traditions, traditional crafts and cuisine, here are my 10 personal favourites in Tokyo (access via the short link below).

www.gomap.de/**toke**

Staying at a ryokan   旅館

One of the highlights of a trip to Japan is a stay at a **traditional inn** known as a *ryokan* (旅館), ideally one with its own hot spring or *onsen* (温泉). The overall experience of a hot bath (etiquette, p. 78), multi-course Japanese evening meal, *kaiseki* (懐石) and sleeping on a *futon* (布団) and *tatami* (畳) in this traditional kind of accommodation is unforgettable. Unfortunately, a one-night stay including half board is not exactly cheap with prices in good quality inns starting at around ¥20,000 per person.

You'll find a futon and tatami are a little harder for sleeping on than a conventional bed, but staff will gladly place two mattresses, *shikibuton* (敷き布団), on top of one another for you. Some ryokan offer Western-style beds. If you would prefer one, you should indicate this when booking. If you still don't feel up to sleeping on the floor, or your holiday budget simply won't stretch to it, you can at least enjoy a few of the advantages of a ryokan without breaking the bank.

If you're mainly interested in experiencing an onsen, many ryokan offer day visitors the chance to use the spa in the afternoon. Once I was at the **Hoshinoyado** in Nikko which can be visited between noon and 3pm for only ¥1000. It is also possible to order various lunchtime **kaiseki menus.** There are also onsen, of course, which cater solely to day visitors, e.g. in **Hakone.** These often have their own restaurant so you can savour the atmosphere of a ryokan as part of a day trip.
www.gomap.de/**rykn**

#Tip: If you're looking for cheap, traditional accommodation in a rural setting, the mostly family-run **guest houses,** *minshuku* (民宿), are a good alternative.

Most menus are written using the Arabic numbers we are familiar with, but some traditional eateries still use **Japanese numbers.** To avoid unpleasant surprises when paying the bill for your meal, it's best to compare the characters.

0:	〇	7:	七
1:	一	8:	八
2:	二	9:	九
3:	三	10:	十
4:	四	100:	百
5:	五	1000:	千
6:	六	10,000:	万
		Yen:	円

Examples:

①	②	③	④	⑤
九十円	六四〇円	三二八〇円	五千円	一万円

①= 90 Yen, ②= 640 Yen, ③= 3280 Yen, ④= 5000 Yen, ⑤=10,000 Yen

Saving money with teishoku 定食

Teishoku (定食) indicates traditional Japanese menus. These always consist of a **main course,** a bowl of **rice,** a bowl of **miso soup** and **pickled vegetables.** A teishoku menu at lunchtime or in the evening provides you with a balanced, healthy meal. Chains such as **Ootoya** or **Yayoiken** offer a wide selection of such complete set menus at reasonable prices, under ¥1000. Here, you choose the main course first, generally fish or chicken with vegetables as a side dish. There is a choice of white rice or a healthier variety with five (Ootoya) or more (Yayoiken) types of grain.
At Yayoiken you can help yourself to white rice as often as you like. At Ootoya, on the other hand, you can order a large portion (350 g) right away at no extra cost. A popular main course at Ootoya is fried chicken with vegetables in a black vinegar sauce. At Yayoiken I like to eat the salted grilled mackerel. Ootoya has menus, or a tablet for electronic ordering, while Yayoiken has machines for ordering at the entrance, both also available in English.
www.gomap.de/**tsku**

#Tip: Prices for lunch and dinner at the teishoku chains are identical, which makes them a cheap alternative in the evening to normal restaurants which normally only offer cut-price menus at lunchtime.

Geisha Level

Once you've worked your way through the steps on this level, you'll be navigating everyday Japanese life with as much elegance and self-confidence as a **geisha** (芸者). Get to know the ins and outs of Japanese infrastructure and how to use it to perfection.

Taking the subway 　　　　　　　　地下鉄

A first glance at the network maps of the **Tokyo** and **Osaka subways,** *chikatetsu* (地下鉄), will leave you feeling overwhelmed by a giant web of countless lines. But don't panic: it's not that difficult to find your way around since every line has been assigned its own colour and letter. What's more, the stations on each line are numbered consecutively. If you struggle with some of the long station names, just watch out for the unique combination of letters and numbers.

Fortunately, in Japan there are no complicated zones, or time based tariff systems as is often the case in Western cities. The price from station A to station B is based on distance, and is a fixed price. The prices are shown on a large network plan. You don't need to bother with that, however, since you're sure to buy a prepaid card from **PASMO, ICOCA, Suica** or another transport company (p. 26). Finding your way through the network of lines is really easy. You just get yourself a route map (PDFs via the link below) or use a practical app (p. 18).

Equipped with single ticket, prepaid card or day ticket, your first test consists of how to get through the ticket barrier. Some barriers are exit-only; watch out for the green arrow. If you have a single ticket or day ticket, you have to find a barrier with a slot, as some barriers nowadays only work with contactless cards and therefore don't have one.

If you have time on the platform, look for the plan which indicates where the exits and changeover points to other lines are located in relation to each train carriage.

That makes it easier for you if you need to change trains at your destination or it helps you avoid battling your way through the rush hour crowds if the exit you want is at the other end of the platform. On the following pages I'll explain how to find the correct exit at your destination.

If you are a man, pay particular attention during the rush hour on work days that you don't get into carriages marked **"Women Only"**. These are indicated by pink stickers on the platform and on the carriage.

The last subway trains run between midnight and 1am, depending on the station. After that, you'll need to get a taxi (p. 64) or simply party till 5am and take the first subway train home.
www.gomap.de/**uban**

#Tip: The question arises again and again: is it worth getting day tickets for the subway? If you already have a JR Pass, you can get to parts of the city (except in Kyoto) using JR lines. For certain places, however, you need the subway. If you've a packed schedule on a particular day, requiring more than four single subway tickets, it's worth investing in a **"Tokyo Subway Ticket"**, which is available for 24, 48 and 72 hours (¥800, 1200 and 1500). These special tourist tickets can only be purchased at a few tourist information offices, ticket offices and shops. In all my trips to Japan I have only ever bought a day ticket once. On a rainy day at the end of September in Tokyo (p. 117).

Reading maps / Finding addresses   住所

The **area maps** at stations are helpful for escaping the rail maze and finding the right exit for your chosen destination. One thing frequently leads to confusion among tourists, however, so I'd like to point it out before we go any further. In contrast to standard Western practice, many maps in Japan are not oriented with North facing up. Instead, they are aligned according to the immediate vicinity. Look which way the North arrow on the map is pointing to avoid walking in the wrong direction. Area maps are usually to be found after the exit ticket barriers. Look here for the correct exit. These are indicated either by a number, an upper-case letter, an upper-case letter *and* a number or sometimes a number with a lower-case letter. On rainy days in particular (p. 116) it's good to know that many department stores can be accessed directly from underground.

At many stations, especially on the subway, it is better to check the maps while still on the platform, as some exits can only be reached by taking a particular staircase from the platform. In Tokyo, for example, large yellow signs even list buildings, museums and shopping centres in English and tell you the appropriate exit to take to get there. The huge Shinjuku station is extremely confusing, having over 50 numbered exits (A1-S3), and is rated the busiest station in the world. There are even two separate A1 exits: on the Ōedo and Marunouchi lines (Shinjuku-Sanchōme station). Fortunately, the exits are one kilometre apart and are in actual fact seldom confused. In addition to the exits, there are staircases numbered 1-20 at the West exit. Staircase 11 has nothing to do with Exit A11, although they are located quite close to each other.

Once you have taken the correct exit, you now need to find your destination by means of its address. Since there are practically no street names in Japan, and the **address,** *jūsho* (住所), system takes a lot of getting used to, I suggest you turn straight away to **Google Maps** or **Apple Maps** and use the telephone number of the destination address (p. 16). At close range, especially in streets lined with skyscrapers, GPS is sometimes not accurate enough. At this point I should also point out that house numbers within a block are usually assigned at random. If you get stuck, the officers at the small **police stations,** *kōban* (交番), are always happy to be of assistance since one of the tasks of the local neighbourhood police is to help you find your way around.

Take as an **example** the address of the Shinjuku Post Office, tel. no.: 03-3340-1086:

〒163-8799 東京都 新宿区 西新宿1–8–8
which translates into
〒163-8799 Tokyo-to, Shinjuku-ku, Nishishinjuku 1-Chōme, 8-8
or 〒163-8799 Tokyo, Shinjuku, Nishishinjuku 1-8-8

Japanese addresses are always written with the largest division first. After the postcode comes the prefecture (Tokyo-to), then the city or ward (Shinjuku-ku), then the city district (Nishishinjuku 1-Chōme). Instead of just 1 for the quarter, you also write 1丁目 *(1-chōme);* the first 8 stands for an entire city block, *banchi,* and finally the last 8 denotes the building number, *gō.* With multi-storey buildings, you also have to make sure that you know the correct floor (B2階, B1階, 1階, 2階 ...).

Using air conditioners エアコン

In large and expensive hotels using the air conditioning is generally quite simple, but that is not always the case in smaller hotels, in Airbnb accommodation or in rural areas. This is because the exclusively Japanese labelling on the remote control makes operation of the **air conditioner,** *aircon* (エアコン), difficult. In reality, you only need three operating elements for adjusting the air conditioning:

運転/停止	On / Off switch
温度	Temperature setting
運転切換	Function button

The function button lets you switch between cooling, heating and other functions.

自動	Automatic
ドライ	Dry
冷房	Cool
暖房	Heat
送風	Ventilator

What are all the other buttons on the remote control for? Well, if the current of air is too strong for your liking, you can adjust it by pressing the [風量] button.

But that's not all: you can change its direction with [風向]. Sometimes there are additional buttons to do this:

上下	Change direction of current up / down
左右	Change direction of current left / right
ワイド	Wide distribution of air

There are a number of different characters for maximum current strength:

パワフル	Powerful
ハイパワー	High power
強風	Strong wind

If you want to have a go at setting the timer, these are the appropriate buttons:

入タイマー	Switch on timer (hours after return)
切タイマー	Switch off timer (overrun in hours)
取消	Cancel timer

If you press [内部クリーン 2秒押し] for longer than two seconds, the internal cleaning function begins. That is really practical in case the unit is emitting a musty smell.

Getting to know konbinis コンビニ

The name **konbini** (コンビニ) derives from "convenience store" and designates the small shops which are open around the clock. The most common of these are **7-Eleven, Lawson, Family-Mart, Daily Yamazaki** or **Mini Stop** and they can be found on every corner. Alongside **food,** ready meals, sandwiches, onigiri, soft drinks, beer, confectionery and sweets, toiletries and other everyday items, they offer many useful services which I much appreciate.

Many shops, for example, have started offering **good coffee,** with prices from ¥110. Just choose the coffee you'd like (or also matcha latte, hot chocolate or tea) from the menu and you'll be handed a paper cup. You won't be asked your first name, like at Starbucks, and you'll have to serve yourself at the machine, but since the beans are freshly ground, and many shops also have tables, chairs and **wi-fi** (p. 20), this is – literally – a small price to pay for the inconvenience.

You can buy not only a reasonably priced breakfast, consisting of coffee, cinnamon rolls, cheesecake, yoghurt and orange juice. Thanks to the water kettle (self-service) and microwave (to be operated by staff only) you can enjoy cheap warm meals such as instant rāmen or fried chicken. **Stew,** *oden* (おでん), is available at the checkout (except during summer).

Other services include making photocopies, sending faxes and printing photos (via memory card) as well as dispatching parcels and luggage (p. 86). A very popular service with the Japanese is the ability to pay electricity, gas and telephone bills, which explains why the queue at the checkout is sometimes a little longer because the customer in front has brought a pile of bills to pay.

I now also get **cash** with my credit card from the **ATMs** in such stores. FamilyMart cooperates with the Japan Post Bank, and 7-Eleven has its own bank. The **Seven Bank** ATMs are even multi-lingual.

Some branches have a machine into which you can pop your dirty shirts. They are laundered and ready for collection again at 9am two days later. To use this service, however, you need to register separately and apply for a customer card.

For other pressing business, many konbinis have toilet facilities for customers. Notes on how to use a high-tech Japanese toilet can be found at the end of this level (p. 66).

Incidentally, the 7-Eleven **photocopiers** can also be used as printers, allowing you to print any document via the internet. However, you'll only find out how that works at Ninja Level (p. 106).

At special terminals you can even buy **entrance tickets** for concerts, museums or amusement parks. This only works for tourists at **Lawson's** Loppi Ticket Machine in English for the Ghibli Museum and Universal Studios. As the operation is somewhat complicated and it is better to book these tickets online before travelling, it is no longer relevant for holidaymakers.

www.gomap.de/**cvst**

#Tip: 7-Eleven now labels onigiri, bentō boxes and other confectionery with information in English. For information on how to recognize the kanji characters of the use-by and best-before date, see the chapter **Budget feasting** on page 95.

Disposing of waste　　　　　　　　ごみ

I come from a nation of supposed world champions when it comes to separating **waste,** *gomi* (ごみ), and it's a fact that the official recycling rate is higher in Germany than in Japan. When I think back over my time in Japan, however, and look at everything which is disposed of in residual waste bins, I am convinced that the Japanese have mastered the art of waste separation but are considerably less skilled at forging statistics!
In Japan, too, paper, cardboard boxes, drinks cans, PET bottles, Tetrapaks, metal and glass are disposed of separately and recycled. For this reason, there are hardly any public refuse bins into which you can simply throw anything.
The best way to dispose of waste on your travels is on railway platforms and at konbinis. Some bins on platforms have a clear window which allows you to see what other people have thrown in. The transparent containers were installed in the wake of the attacks by the Ōmu-Shinrikyō sect in the 1990s. Immediately afterwards, many had been sealed or removed completely. You usually find three or four different containers marked with corresponding symbols or even signs in English. If not, here are the Japanese designations to help you:

カン	Drinks cans
ビン	Glass bottles
ペットボトル	PET bottles
新聞・雑誌	Newspapers and magazines (paper)
その他のゴミ	Residual waste

There are often no containers for waste paper in **konbinis.** After all, why would you throw away a newspaper you have just bought? Instead, there is a residual waste bin marked [もやせるゴミ], which translates as "combustible waste". So everything which does not belong in the other containers and which is in some way combustible, such as packaging and food scraps, is thrown in here. That is a rough explanation of the Japanese waste disposal concept. Everything which cannot be recycled simply but rather incinerated in some way ends up in one of the city's large waste incineration plants. Occasionally, the containers for plastic bottles have a second small opening for the bottle tops which are disposed of separately.

But what do you do with your waste if there is no station or konbini nearby? At food stalls, for example, if there is no bin I simply hand the waste back in there. There are sometimes bins next to **drinks machines** for collecting empty cans and containers only. Otherwise I take my waste back to the hotel with me or, at lunchtime, ask at the restaurant if I can leave it there.

#Tip: Even when you buy, for example, a can of lemonade or a bottle of water at a konbini, it will be packed in a bag for you. If you want to **avoid waste** and are paying at the checkout for something you want to consume immediately, you can say, *"Sono mama de ii desu",* "That's fine like that, thank you", or even clearer, *"fukuro wa irimasen",* "I don't need a bag". A sticker on the item indicates that you have paid for it. Plastic bags are now charged (¥3 or ¥5).

To smoke or not to smoke? 喫煙/禁煙

If you are a smoker, you don't have to freeze in the cold in winter, as many small restaurants and bars do not have a no-smoking rule. However, a stricter law came into force in Tokyo in April 2020, which only allows smoking in designated smoking rooms. Only small family-run restaurants without staff are exempt from the new stricter regulations.

Smoking on the street is also already banned in many urban areas in Japan. To find out whether smoking is prohibited or not in a particular street, look out for the signs erected close to railway stations; some feature maps showing streets where smoking is banned marked in red. Often these are heavily frequented streets or shopping centres. The current fine for smoking in such streets is ¥2000. Sometimes this is even indicated by stickers on the pavement. Discarding cigarette ends is not allowed anywhere.

The best idea is to buy yourself a **pocket ashtray,** *keitai haizara* (携帯灰皿), in a 100 Yen Shop (p. 98). The Japanese tobacco industry is financing an extensive image campaign to encourage its customers to be more considerate. The aim is to completely eradicate the risks arising from passive smoking and discarded cigarette ends in public spaces. The fact that the Japanese state still holds a third of shares in **Japan Tobacco** certainly plays a role here. Smokers are allowed to smoke only in designated areas in inner cities or use sponsored lounges. Smoking is prohibited in all areas of railway stations. During my time as a student here, work colleagues used to gather behind a shower curtain at the office window during their cigarette break. In the meantime, offices and stations have closed high-tech cabins with filter systems.

If you need to buy cigarettes while in Japan, the best place to go is to a konbini (p. 56), as purchasing from a vending machine requires you to prove your age by means of a special ID card.

Unfortunately, smoking is still widespread in many small restaurants – much to the annoyance of non-smokers. Some restaurants ban smoking at lunchtimes, and fortunately there are an increasing number of eateries which have banned smoking altogether, not least to protect their staff. If you wish to avoid smoke entirely, you should not visit an izakaya (p. 112). Many large coffee chains have separate areas for smokers and non-smokers. In city centres, these are often a last place of refuge for smokers. Although these used to be larger and often more attractively furnished than the non-smoking sections, this is gradually beginning to change. Many smoking sections are now on a different floor, or behind a glassed off area. Unfortunately this does not always stop clouds of smoke occasionally wafting across to the non-smokers area. The only chain that is 100% non-smoking inside is Starbucks, however, other chains are beginning to have stores which are entirely smoke free. When inside smoking is prohibited, it is sometimes allowed outside branches, e.g. in Osaka.

www.gomap.de/**rhnr**

#Tip: If you would like a **non-smoking seat,** *kinenseki* (禁煙席), or a **smoking seat,** *kitsuenseki* (喫煙席), you should ask or point to these signs, as appropriate.

Appreciating service サービス

Service (サービス) is taken seriously in Japan, and the customer is truly king and treated almost like a god. I have put together a few examples to illustrate the concept of service:
Many **restaurants** make choosing your meal easier by providing plastic models of the food on the menu. **Water** or **green tea** is available free of charge and brought to the table together with the menu. You will even find mouthwash provided in some toilets and restrooms so you can freshen your breath after eating.
If you get up to go and forget one of your belongings, you usually won't even get as far as the door as the attentive staff check for such eventualities as a matter of routine. You pay for your meal at the checkout as you leave the restaurant. No tiresome hanging around for the service personnel to arrive with your bill.
In **rainy weather** you will find umbrella dryers inside the entrance to shops or a device which wraps your wet umbrella in a plastic sheath. Checkout counters often have a hook or rail for customers to hang up their umbrella so they have their hands free when paying. Clear markings on the ground show you where to **queue** for something.
In **shops** it is standard practice to elaborately wrap purchases – or also as gifts, if you wish. If you buy a small cake, you will be asked how long your journey home will take. An ice pack is then popped into the bag if necessary. Dry ice is sometimes provided with take-away ice-cream, although this entails an extra charge, depending on the shop. Japanese **hotel rooms** are always equipped with a kettle and free tea and coffee.

One evening in front of the railway station in Fukushima I noticed **taxis** with two drivers. Due to the zero-alcohol level for car drivers, you can have yourself driven home in your own car with the taxi following behind to bring the driver back to the taxi stand again.

A lot of thought goes into **product packaging** design, too. The yoghurt pots with fold-up spoons inside the lid come to mind here. Onigiri, snacks made of rice and seaweed, are artistically wrapped but can still be unpacked easily and the plastic wrap separating rice and dried seaweed removed without the rice sticking to your fingers.

Great products which make life easier also reflect this emphasis on service and customer orientation. I particularly like buying **stationery** and **travel accessories** in Japan. There are pencil cases with an elastic band which lets you fasten them to note books so they don't get lost. Garment compression bags, which reduce the amount of space your clothes take up in your suitcase, are now also available from the Japanese chain, **MUJI,** which has branches and online shops in many countries.

www.gomap.de/**srvc**

#Tip: At the DIY chain **HANDS** you can purchase wooden signs and seals on which common Western first names are written onomatopoeically in kanji. If your name isn't available, you can have one made there or at a machine at one of the **Don Quijote** stores (p. 99). My favourites, however, are the personal seals from **Shinimonogurui** (p. 128).

Taking a taxi   タクシー

There are a lot of **taxis** (タクシー) in Japan; they supplement the dense public transport network and are even on hand when the last subway and other trains have departed at around midnight.
You only have to stand on the kerb and raise your hand briefly and in next to no time your personal driver will be ready and waiting. In very busy areas, you need to go to a taxi stand. As if by magic, the driver uses a special mechanism to open the rear door on the left for you to get in.

If there's a sudden shower or a typhoon is expected, there is an acute shortage of taxis for hire, which are recognisable, by the way, by the characters [空車] lit up in red. The driver of a seemingly unoccupied taxi may not stop for foreigners for fear of not being able to make himself understood. Sadly, not all aspects of the service concept have embedded themselves in the minds of taxi drivers.

Not all taxis accept credit cards, so be sure to have enough **cash** with you especially on long journeys. For short trips taxis are not at all expensive, with tariffs starting at around ¥500-730. After 10pm there is a surcharge of 20%. Don't expect the taxi driver to be particularly familiar with the area. Instead you should have with you the address of your destination written in Japanese on a piece of paper. Alternatively, it's usually enough to enter the telephone number (p. 16) in the taxi's sat nav. Don't expect to be driven directly to the door in narrow streets either, or to be helped with loading and unloading your luggage. As a rule, tipping is not customary in Japan, although I report on the following pages on the one exception I experienced as an expat.

The first time I returned to Japan from Germany, loaded down with luggage, I didn't take a taxi. Instead I used the orange Airport Limousine Bus to a hotel in Shinagawa. At the hotel there was the usual long queue of parked taxis, with drivers hoping to pick up a lucrative fare after their long wait. There I was, a foreigner with several suitcases, wanting to be driven not even two kilometres up the hill to my apartment. The driver stubbed out his cigarette, carefully preserving it for later, having quite unexpectedly helped me to put my heavy pieces of luggage into the boot. When I gave him the not too distant address, I heard him swearing under his breath as he lost his composure. At the end of our five-minute drive to my accommodation, the only way I was able to remedy the situation was by consciously breaching the widely publicised unwritten rule: "You do not give tips in Japan". So, with a smile, I pushed back the plastic tray held out by the driver and containing my change of ¥400 and said, *"Tabacco no okane desu"*, which means something like "Please, buy yourself some tobacco". The driver's stony expression vanished in an instant, and I found myself staring into a smiling face again.
www.gomap.de/**taxi**

#Tip: If something similar should happen to you and you are not sure whether the driver smokes, the right way to turn down your change is to say, *"Otsuri wa kekkō desu"*, "Please keep the change".

Using the toilet correctly　　　トイレ

Compared to Berlin, for example, Tokyo and in fact Japan as a whole, is a veritable paradise where public **toilets** (トイレ / お手洗い / 化粧室) are concerned. You'll generally find free toilet facilities behind the barriers at every **train** and **subway station,** in **department stores** and **public parks.** These are generally clean, and the cleaning staff are well paid and for this reason not dependent on tips.

While large department stores do not usually have toilets on every floor, they are to be found in the basement and on floors where there is a restaurant. What's more, all konbinis have at least one toilet and you won't be frowned upon if you need to use it without purchasing anything. I have never come across locked toilets in Japan for which it is necessary to ask staff at the checkout for the key.

In 95% of cases, separate toilet facilities for men and women are usually recognisable by colour or symbol. At the **coffee chain Tsubakiya** and in rural areas, however, it can be useful to distinguish between the following kanji:

男子用 or 男性用	Men	紳士用	Gentlemen
女子用 or 女性用	Women	婦人用	Ladies

The old squat toilets are still in use, but you generally find Western-style toilets too. Look out for a sign saying 洋式 on the door of the stall. If there is no Western-style toilet, for example in a ryokan, you usually only have to try another floor.

A Japanese invention, the high-tech "Washlets" (ウォシュレット), are equipped with heated seats – very pleasant in winter – and cleansing water jets.

The most important button for stopping any function immediately is
止　　Stop

If you are only searching for the right button to flush with:
大 or 流す大　　"Large" flush
小 or 流す小　　"Small" flush

おしり　　Water jet for the rear, pale blue with stylised buttocks
ビデ　　Water jet for the front, pink symbol representing a woman
マイルド or やわらか For a gentle rinse

You can adjust the pressure of the water jet with 水勢 or 洗浄強さ:
強 higher　　　　弱 lower

For sensitive noses and ears, use the following buttons:
脱臭　　Deodorise
音姫　　The "sound princess", ***otohime,*** masks very personal sounds; usually only in ladies' toilets

Frequently there are buttons, [洗浄位置], for pointing the water jet in every direction imaginable, though I would advise you to simply point your posterior in the direction of the jet!

Some premium models have additional functions:
マッサージ　　Massage with pulsating water jet
乾燥　　　　　Dryer for drying without paper

#Note: More buttons are often hidden behind a panel or appear as grey ones at the rear. They are for programming and cleaning, so you'd better not touch!

Changing shoes

It is not permitted to enter traditional inns, **ryokan,** private houses and also some smaller museums wearing outdoor shoes. Visitors and guests are given slippers which are almost always too small for Western feet. Even in some offices, employees change their **shoes,** *kutsu* (靴). I can still remember the embarrassing fluffy slippers my boss used to wear at the time I did my internship semester.

In a ryokan, the rice straw mats, *tatami,* may not even be walked on wearing slippers. These are to be removed on the step at the entrance.

Similarly, it is also forbidden to use the toilet wearing normal slippers. Special toilet slippers are provided for this purpose. The only difference is in the colour, usually red, and the word "toilet" printed on them which make them instantly recognisable.

#Tip: Before changing your slippers, place yours in front of the toilet so that you can't fail to notice them when you leave. Otherwise you might commit the same faux pas as I did on my first visit to a private house. When leaving the toilet, I forgot to change my shoes again and found myself suddenly standing in my hosts' living room wearing the toilet slippers.

Samurai Level

The warrior noblemen, the **samurai** (侍), played a key role in feudal Japan. In this level, I' like to help you with a few things you might not have had the courage to attempt. It's time to demonstrate the same courage as a samurai!

Collecting stamps 御朱印所

If you plan to visit numerous shrines and temples on your trip, a pilgrim's book is a great souvenir. It also gives you the opportunity to get in touch with the monks. Firstly, you buy a so-called **goshuin-chō** (御朱印所) on site. It is a small book with sheets of relatively thick paper folded like an accordion. A goshuin-chō usually contains space for 24 **goshuin** (御朱印) – stamps combined with calligraphy made by the monks. A goshuin-chō costs with the first stamp ¥1,000-2,000 and for each additional entry at other shrines and temples you usually pay ¥500. This amount is seen as a donation, by the way, and it is customary to say thank you and bow when you receive your pilgrim's book back after a short wait.

To find the counter for goshuin, look for the [御朱印] sign. Sometimes there are different stamps to choose from and you have to pick one unless you want to spend money on several.

Since the **COVID-19 pandemic,** for reasons of hygiene there is often only goshuin on a single sheet, which you then stick into your booklet. It's best to stick the sheets in at the hotel in the evening before you lose them or mix them up. Glue sticks are available in every 100 yen shop (p. 98) or in the konbini (p. 56); if you are staying in a luxury hotel, you can get such stationery from the concierge.

#Tip: If you are afraid of the time and expense, you can collect the lovely free stamps that are available at railway stations and at most sights and museums.

In Japan, you will often find **rubber stamps** and ink pads in a corner of many sights and railway stations, which visitors can use to stamp a piece of paper or a notebook as a souvenir. The stamps at railway stations are usually somewhat smaller, while there are larger stamps with elaborate motifs and dates at tourist attractions. In the botanical garden of Kōchi, stamps in different colours were placed in several locations. Together on a sheet of paper, this resulted in a multi-coloured picture of the botanist *Makino*.

To create your own travel diary without much effort, I have published the **Japan Hanko** book with space for 120 stamps. At the front is a numbered overview table to enter the place and date of each stamp. Then there are sheets with enough space for 84 souvenir stamps. Because ink tends to bleed through the paper on some stamps, the reverse has been left blank so that it can be used for notes. 36 station stamps *ekistanpu* (駅スタンプ) can be added at the end. Japan Hanko has the same format as this book and can be ordered from Amazon at the same price as this book.
www.gomap.de/**japh**

#Tip: Shrines and temples also often have free seals that you can put in your booklet. However, under no circumstances should you use your pilgrim's book for this, as it is only intended for the paid stamps and monks may refuse to enter further goshuin. True stamp fans therefore always carry two stamp books with them, some even three, to distinguish between Buddhist temples, Shinto shrines and souvenir stamps.

Booking cars and driving 車

If you would like to drive when in Japan, you need to remember to apply for an **International Driving Permit (IDP)** in your home country as part of your travel preparations. Visitors from Germany, France, Belgium, Switzerland and Taiwan require their national driving licence with a translation instead of an IDP.

A **car,** *kuruma* (車) is very practical especially for remote places, so I will explain here how you can get a rental car. Car rental companies with a wide network of branches and booking procedures in English include **Nippon Rent a Car** as well as the car rental subsidiaries of manufacturers **Toyota** and **Nissan.**

JR Rent-A-Car is sometimes a worthwhile option as you can get a 10% discount on car hire if you have a Japan Rail Pass.

At car rental pick-up points in rural areas you are unlikely to come across English-speaking staff. They usually make do with bilingual **"Check Sheets"** which you have to sign. But you won't get anywhere without the respective International Driving Permit or your licence and passport. As a rule, you have to provide an address and telephone number in Japan, so use those of your hotel. If you are prone to leaving possessions behind in rental cars, it's a good idea to leave the contact details of the hotel you will be staying in *after* returning your vehicle.

You will be offered the chance, as usual, to reduce the insurance excess in the event of damage (often ¥100,000) for a relatively high additional fee. Decide for yourself which of the long list of exceptions in the small print makes sense for you. Should you get a parking ticket, it would be better to pay the fine yourself at the nearest police station, as car rental companies generally charge excessive lump sums in this case! If you are unfamiliar with driving on the left, you'll get used to it fairly quickly. The fact that all rental cars have automatic transmission also makes life easier.

Drivers of left-hand drive cars should remember to check the windscreen wiper and indicator levers; you might find that they are "the other way round" compared to your own car. That way you avoid washing your windscreen when turning a corner!

The first major hurdle for me was parking the car, because I initially had trouble getting the key out of the ignition. I subsequently discovered that in a Toyota Vitz this is only possible if you depress the ignition lock after turning.

Sat navs in rental cars sometimes have an English-language version, but in most cases the menus are in Japanese only. The most important button for getting to the main menu is [メニュー]. It's difficult entering addresses in Japanese, but there is a feature which lets you find the sights, hotels and restaurants by their telephone number. Make sure when planning your trip that you write down these numbers. The menu item for this feature is [電話番号] and is also marked with a telephone symbol.

The speed limit on overland roads is between 50 and 60 km/h (31-37 mph) and on motorways between 80 and 100 km/h (50-62 mph), however many Japanese drivers go approximately 10-20 km/h faster than permitted. If you do the same, I accept no liability for this!

www.gomap.de/**cars**

#Tip: When travelling in rural areas, I always book my car at a car rental service located at the railway station which is closest to my destination and still easy to reach by express train from Tokyo. Due to the high motorway tolls and the speed limits it makes little sense to begin a long drive in Tokyo or Osaka. Besides, this way you can avoid the possibly unfamiliar experience of having to drive on the left in a big city!

Conforming to etiquette　　　　気配り

Entire books fill the broad subject of Japanese etiquette. To help you understand how Japanese society works, I've summarised a few **important rules** below: You will notice that **mutual respect and consideration,** *kikubari* (気配り), are a stronger characteristic of everyday life here than in the West. Rules, for example stipulating the observance of red traffic lights, standing on the left and walking on the right on escalators, switching your phone to silent mode and not speaking on the telephone on the train, not raising your voice in public, not wearing overpowering perfumes, always queuing correctly and not barging to the front, are respected by all and strictly adhered to.

People unselfishly put the needs of others before their own so as not to jeopardise the **harmony** of the group. Punctuality is extremely important and means that you should generally arrive between 5 and 10 minutes before the agreed time. It is considered acceptable and necessary to allow a little time to spare when travelling by public transport, in case you happen to miss your subway connection.

Long before the **COVID-19 pandemic,** many people **wear a mask** over their mouth and nose in public if they have a cold or flu so as not to infect others. In spring and summer, however, it is often hay fever sufferers who wear them as a pollen filter.

When **greeting** or **saying goodbye** to someone, it is customary to bow rather than shake hands. The deeper the bow, the more polite it is. Even for Japanese people meeting for the first time, it is therefore difficult to gauge the correct depth of the bow. As a tourist, you won't be expected to bow; just do what you think is right. Sometimes, more cosmopolitan Japanese people will shake hands as a greeting.

It can be helpful to have plenty of **business cards** with you so you can exchange them when making an important contact. You should hold your card in both hands when presenting it. Do not simply put any card you are given in your pocket or write anything on it in the presence of the giver. It is best to look at the card for a few moments. Close **physical contact** in public is not customary – even lovers do not kiss in public and only rarely are seen holding hands. Eating is so important in Japan that it is not done casually, for example when walking along the street or on public transport. Celebrations, *matsuri* (祭り), and shinkansen (p. 88) are the exception. Wherever you go in Japan, you may be surprised to find people sniffling. This is because **blowing your nose** loudly is frowned on, whereas it is normal to sniffle instead. This is however beginning to change, and young Japanese people are more likely to try and discretely blow their nose than sniff continuously. If you need to blow your nose, you are unlikely to offend unless it is done particularly loudly.

#Tip: It's the exception that proves the rule: On **escalators** in the Kansai region you stand on the right and walk on the left. It is said that this goes back to the days when merchants in Osaka carried their purses on the right-hand side to protect against theft, while the samurai in Tokyo wore their swords on the left and drew them with their right hand. There was no such thing as an escalator in those days, of course, but the rule applies to walking on pavements, too. In actual fact, the organisers of the Expo 1970 in Osaka wanted to put on an international, cosmopolitan face and hurriedly introduced this rule which has held to this day. Attempts are even being made to prohibit walking on escalators altogether because of the risk of accidents, but few are following this new rule.

Rules for photographers　　　　　　　写真

It's a well-known fact that the Japanese love to take **photos, shashin** (写真), on their travels; most tourists in Japan are just as keen photographers. If you would like to photograph individual people, you should always make this known and ask if it is OK to do so. Alongside this globally accepted rule, there are a few other things to be aware of when taking photographs in Japan:

Large crowds, for example at the famous Shibuya junction in Tokyo, are popular photo motifs, but you should take care that the **faces of people** in the foreground are not clearly recognisable if you are intending to publish the picture. If your photo contains a recognisable image of an adulterous couple, you could be sued under Japanese law in any possible ensuing divorce proceedings. Admittedly, this is highly unlikely, but such cases have been known to occur. Do not point a **telephoto lens** at children or women's bare legs. This could be construed as voyeurism. The same accusation could be made of someone taking **photos using a mobile phone** which makes no audible noise.

Taking photographs of famous Japanese people in public is allowed, but publication of such images without permission is generally forbidden. That's bad news for paparazzi and good news for personal rights. Watch out for **prohibition signs** in areas where there are lots of tourists, in museums, shrines and temples. Occasionally, certain things are generally prohibited. This may just be a ban on flash photography, or on the use of **selfie sticks** where large crowds gather, for example at New Year at the Meiji Shrine or on railway platforms. Incidentally, it is forbidden to use camera tripods in the grounds of the Meiji Shrine. **Staff** at food or souvenir stalls understandably don't want to be photographed by thousands of tourists all day.

If you really want to take a photo, however, it's quite simple. Buy something at the stall and, as you pay, ask politely if you may take a picture: *"Shashin o tottemo ī desu ka?"* So far, I have hardly ever been turned down by a stallholder.

Women in maid's costumes, for example when distributing advertising material for a maid café, generally prefer not to be photographed, regardless of whether you ask permission or not. Many years ago, while I was taking some pictures on a street in Akihabara, one such maid got really angry with me because she thought I had photographed her. She insisted that I show her the pictures I had taken on the camera display and delete them if necessary. Even inside maid cafés you are not allowed to take photographs of people, though for a small fee you may have a Polaroid taken with one of the maids. Now, after that list of don'ts, here's some information on what you *can* do:

You may photograph your food in a **restaurant,** as long as other diners are not in the picture. Street artists usually have no objection to being photographed, except for **cosplayers,** who should always be asked first. Some cosplayers in Harajuku like having their picture taken, others are strictly against it and are so irritated by the many tourists that they even carry a "No photo" sign around with them.

#Tip: In the temple area of Asakusa in Tokyo or at the Fushimi-Inari Shrine in Kyoto, many of the women you'll see wearing traditional costume are not actually Japanese, but tourists from other Asian countries. Some are happy to have their photograph taken by strangers, others are in a hurry because the deadline for handing in their hired kimono is due or their tour bus is waiting.

Bathing at a sentō 銭湯

There are a number of rules to be observed in public bathhouses, **sentō** (銭湯), or hot springs, **onsen** (温泉), which differ from ones Western visitors may be used to. Nevertheless, the experience of visiting a traditional public bathhouse is not to be missed. There used to be one in every neighbourhood, as only few people had the luxury of their own bath at home. Although there has been something of a revival of this kind of bathing culture in recent years, the number of bathhouses is still falling because proprietors often can't find anyone to take over when they retire. The famous **Koshino-yu** in Azabu-Jūban has now disappeared, though the nearby **Takeno-yu** bathhouse closed for a while and then thankfully re-opened.

You can recognise a bathhouse by the letters **yu** (ゆ) in the name. Most sentō open in the late afternoon, so I headed off to **Takeno-yu** at around 4pm I removed my outdoor shoes immediately at the entrance and put them in a locker and left my heavy camera bag in one of the larger ones nearby. At the counter, however, I was told that the lockers were intended for shoes only – and the larger ones for boots – and that each visitor was only entitled to use one locker. So I removed my camera bag from the locker, paid the entrance fee of ¥520 and borrowed a small towel for ¥50 (large towel, ¥200). There are usually more lockers in the changing room where you can leave your bag, valuables and your clothes. If you have long hair, you should tie it back or pin it up. It is customary to bathe naked in a sentō, although you may use the small towel to cover yourself up while walking around. The baths are normally gender segregated; only the outdoor pools, **rotenburo** (露天風呂), in rural areas are occasionally mixed.

The most important thing when bathing in Japan is to wash yourself before entering the water. To do this, you take a small stool at the entrance and soap yourself sitting down. There are taps and mirrors along the walls, and shower gel, shampoo, conditioner, shaving foam and disposable razors are also available. Small tubs are provided so you can mix the water to the right temperature before pouring it over yourself to rinse off the soap. You can use the shower head to do this, but you should be careful not to splash others with water in the process. The small towel is also used for washing with, but should never be taken into the bath itself. Either leave it lying on the side of the pool or place it, folded, on your head. The water in the pool is hotter than you are used to at home, so I recommend either taking some time to acclimatise, by pouring hot water over yourself from the tub, or by stepping into the pool very slowly. Once you're in the water, it's pure relaxation. Close your eyes and enjoy the silence. Before returning to the changing room, you dry yourself off as best you can so as to avoid getting the floor of the changing room wet.

#Tip: **Tattoos** are often taboo in Japanese baths. If your tattoo is small, don't ask first, just cover it up with a waterproof plaster or sports (kinesio) tape. People with larger tattoos have to find a bathhouse which allows them. A list of these can be found on the website of the organisation, **"Tattoo Friendly".**
www.gomap.de/**snto**

Understanding gestures   仕草

The use of gestures in Japan differs in some aspects from Western customs and can easily lead to misunderstandings. My most confusing moment occurred at the beginning of my first stay in Japan, when my boss asked me to come to him. He reached out his hand and started flapping it up and down. To me, it looked as if he was shooing me away or waving goodbye.

In large crowds, elderly gentlemen in particular like to bend their arm and move the flat of their hand in front of their face. This resembles someone trying to clear a path through undergrowth using a samurai sword. But that's not what it's all about; it's simply a way of not having to say *"Sumimasen",* "Excuse me, may I get past, please?"

Where we use an **"X"** to check boxes when filling in forms, in Japan an **"O"** is often used. In Japan, **"X"** also means "incorrect" and **"O"** means "correct". You also make the corresponding signs with your fingers or arms. So, if you see someone signalling to you with their forearms crossed in front of their chest, you are doing something forbidden and you ought to stop.

The Japanese express **agreement** by nodding their head, but like any "yes", it can simply mean that they have heard what you're saying. **Disagreement** is indicated by a vigorous waving of the hand in front of the face. The common OK sign in the West, in which a circle is formed between thumb and index finger, is used by some young males. If they remain silent with the palm of their hand facing upwards, this is an impolite gesture signifying money and could be misunderstood.

To make it clear you are talking about yourself, *watashi,* you usually touch your nose with your index finger. If you are referring to someone you don't know, you can say *anata,* while indicating the person using the flat of your hand. Pointing a finger at others is considered rude in Japan and shows bad manners. Showing someone the way, as in **"This way, please",** is done by extending the arm with the palm of the hand facing upwards.

The **V-sign** familiar in the West has little to do with victory, but is nowadays often used to mean **"peace",** when posing for a photo with friends. If the sign is used when entering a restaurant, it is a request for a table for two. For groups of up to ten people, read below.

#Tip: Indicating numbers and **counting** with the fingers is different in Japan. You use the following system to communicate a number to someone else, for example, the number of drinks you want to order: turn your palm outwards and show the required number of fingers. Here, the index finger means **one** and the index finger plus middle finger mean **two.** To indicate **six,** you lay the index finger of one hand on the palm of the other hand. Add more fingers for counting to **nine.** As in the West, showing your outstretched palms indicates **ten.** When the Japanese are counting to themselves, they only use one hand. They begin with the hand open and, beginning with the thumb, fold down each finger until they get to five. From six upwards, the fingers are extended again, beginning with the little finger.

Opening doors ドア

Even opening a simple **door,** *doa* (ドア), in a restaurant or small shop can be a challenge in Japan. In large department stores and restaurants, it's not a problem as they generally have automatic doors which, with very few exceptions, open so quickly that there's no danger of you crashing into the glass pane if you walk at normal walking pace. Traditional old houses and smaller restaurants often have **sliding doors** which you must push to one side. These obviously have no handle, only an inset door pull for your fingers. The real problem, however, is with sliding doors which look like conventional doors. Usually these are glass doors with an aluminium frame and a large handle.

It happened to me again on my last Japan trip. I pushed and pulled the handle – nothing happened. Then I tried using a little more force; perhaps the door was just not running smoothly. Eventually, the waiter inside the restaurant noticed me and pushed the door to one side with a friendly smile.

#Tip: Before you tear a supposedly open door, which is in fact locked, off its hinges, here are the two most important signs which will indicate whether a shop or restaurant is currently open or closed:

営業中 or 商い中	open
準備中	closed

Incidentally, there is one distinctive feature of the doors to some **toilet stalls** you need to be aware of. Old wooden doors and even some modern designer variations often do not have an "occupied" sign, and there is no lock visible from the outside. Generally, doors and partition walls also go right down to the floor, so it is not possible to take a peek underneath for a telltale pair of shoes! If you are unsure as to whether a stall is occupied or not, just knock on the door twice. If there is someone on the other side, they will also knock twice from the inside to indicate "yes, this toilet is occupied!"

Uncertainty on this point of etiquette was the undoing of a member of the board of a large cooperation based in Stuttgart, Germany. In an expensive restaurant he found himself in a traditional squat toilet whose door did not close properly. Consequently, he had to hold the door closed himself. As if that wasn't enough, there then came a knock at the door! The automatic reaction of the executive, who was not entirely familiar with Japanese customs, was to hold onto the door even tighter and to try and finish his "business" as quietly as possible. The Japanese gentleman on the other side – a regular visitor to the restaurant – knew about the problem with the door and, after waiting a moment, took a run up and charged into it. It's not hard to imagine how this particular "business" situation panned out. Following this rather unfortunate encounter, the planned collaboration no longer took place under a lucky star.

Taking the bus   バス

It's best to get your first taste of bus travel in a large city like **Tokyo.** As soon as you have found the bus stop and got on at the front of the **bus,** *basu* (バス), with the correct number, you must pay the fare of ¥210. This is a flat fare, regardless of how far you travel. On municipal buses you pay either with a prepaid card (p. 26) or in cash. The drivers' machine only gives change for notes worth a maximum of ¥1000. At your destination you get off at the back. In contrast to journeys made with trains, the subway and other buses, you don't need to use your prepaid card to touch out. In most other cities, such as **Kyoto** or **Osaka,** you get on at the back and pay at the machine at the front as you get off. On some heavily frequented tourist routes in Kyoto (flat fare ¥230) passengers now get on at the front, as in Tokyo.

In autumn I visited Hiraizumi in Iwate Prefecture. Accustomed as I was to bus travel in Tokyo, however, I incurred the rage of the local driver. I correctly got on the bus at the back and pulled a **small piece of paper with a number on it** from the machine.

Outside town, fares are calculated by the distance travelled. Your fare is displayed on a screen at the front next to your ticket number and increases as your journey continues. Near the driver there was a fibreglass box with a slot. Following the example of the other passengers, I threw my bit of paper and my money into the slot and watched it fall onto a small conveyor belt. What I didn't know, however, was that you were supposed to insert the correct amount of money, which is why the enraged driver had to dismantle his machine in order to extract my money and give me my change.

By chance, the same driver was behind the wheel on my return journey, so I decided to make a special effort to use the correct slot this time. There was in fact a second small coin slot into which I threw my fare of ¥260 in the form of three ¥100 coins, hoping to receive ¥40 change. To my surprise, a vast quantity of small change came pouring out of the machine: three ¥50 coins and fifteen ¥10 coins landed in the tray. This slot is only to be used for changing money (¥500 or ¥100 coins). There is a separate slot for changing ¥1000 notes. Like I said, you must always pay the exact amount. As a tourist you'll probably get away with holding out a handful of coins to the driver and letting him pick out the fare. When I return in a few years' time, I hope the old buses will have been equipped with contactless payment devices like the buses in Hakone. Here, when getting on and off the bus, you just touch the reader with your prepaid card; it's as simple as that. You only need to ensure your card is charged with enough money beforehand.

#Tip: If you're planning to take more than two bus rides in one day in Tokyo, it's worth buying a "One-day Pass" from Toei Bus, **"Ichinichi Jōshaken",** for ¥500. To pay in cash, you have to buy these at the ticket office. With a prepaid card, you get on the bus and say, *"Ichinichi jōshaken o-negai shimasu"* and touch the marking when told to do so. From then on this flat fare entitles you to use all municipal buses for the whole day.
www.gomap.de/**tbus**

Forwarding suitcases   宅急便

Back in 1993 after my first flight to Japan I got to know the much-used **forwarding service, *takkyūbin*** (宅急便), for transporting your **luggage, *nimotsu*** (荷物). An employee from the personnel department of the company where I was due to do my six-month internship semester was waiting to meet me at Narita airport. After exchanging greetings, the first step was to go to a counter where I had to fill in a number of forms and hand in my large suitcase. The journey from the airport to the small town in Saitama Prefecture, involving various trains and a lot of connections, would have been quite a challenge with my heavy suitcase in tow. The suitcase was delivered directly to my new apartment the next morning.

Unless you take the **Airport Limousine Bus** direct to your hotel or pluck up the courage to use **public transport** to the city centre, this service is really useful. Travelling with lots of luggage on the train or subway is really only feasible at the weekend or outside the rush hour.

If you travel around Japan a lot, a small suitcase or rucksack is the simplest option as you can stow it within reach on the luggage rack – even on the Shinkansen. Should you be travelling with heavy bags, bear in mind that many older stations or ones in rural areas do not have lifts, even in a country like Japan with its ultra-modern public transport network. Where long journeys with large suitcases are unavoidable, I leave these at my last hotel before going on short excursions or use a **locker** at the station, though this is only possible for a maximum of one or three days at major stations. Newer lockers now operate with prepaid cards (p. 26); for the older ones you need ¥100 coins.

If you are not returning to your original destination, you can also have your luggage forwarded from one hotel to another in the same way as from the airport. In case an inexpensive hotel does not offer this service, you can simply hand in your luggage at the next **konbini** (p. 56).

The forwarding company, **Kuroneko Yamato,** is recognisable by its logo of a black cat carrying its young. "Kuroneko" means "black cat" and "Yamato" is the company name. Yamato is the largest provider of this service, which is also aimed at foreign tourists under the name „**Hand-Free Travel**". **Sagawa Express** markets its service under „**Sightseeing Without Baggage**".

You can also use the forwarding service on your return journey, although in this case you should send your luggage from the hotel at least two days before your departure. Forwarding between hotels usually takes less than a day.

www.gomap.de/**gpkt**

#Tip: To use the luggage delivery service, simply ask at the hotel reception if this service is offered. In more expensive hotels, they will probably even help you fill out the form. In cheaper hotels with less staff, they will probably just hand you the form and you have to fill it out by yourself. This is also possible in English, but you should write very readable and only in block letters. A large suitcase up to 25 kg costs ¥2,510 for transport within Tokyo and ¥2,630 for transport from Tokyo to Kyoto at Yamato. A small cabin suitcase up to 15 kg costs ¥1,850 and ¥1,970 respectively. Yamato's English website contains detailed price and size tables.

Feasting on the train   弁当

Earlier on in the book, I told you that people don't eat on public transport. Well, there is one big exception, namely journeys on the **Shinkansen** bullet trains and lengthier express train journeys to popular holiday destinations such as Nikko. On the Shinkansen, there's enough space between you and your neighbour even in 2nd class compartments to make this train journey more of a private experience which allows you to behave as such. So why not kick off your shoes and enjoy a nap? Or buy some dried meat and fish and a few cans of beer for your colleagues, so you can celebrate sealing that deal on the way back from a visit to a customer? I've seen and done all this and more on my many journeys through Japan. As standard, however, the Japanese are kitted out with at least a lunch box, known as a **bentō** (弁当), and a bottle of green tea. So before you embark on a long train journey, I suggest you leave yourself enough time to buy a station bentō, **eki-ben** (駅弁).

The selection at Tokyo station is huge, because it is the main Shinkansen station, so allow an extra 15 minutes. If you are short on time, you can also buy a bentō and drinks from the service personnel on the Tōkaidō-Shinkansen, but nowadays only in 1st class (Green Car) on the *Hikari* and *Nozomi*. Passengers in 2nd class can still buy coffee and ice cream from the vending machine on the platform shortly before the journey.

#Tip: If you are travelling to **Nikko** in the morning, I advise you to buy your breakfast, bentō or drink at a konbini (p. 56). Sadly, the selection at Tōbu-Asakusa station is limited, and there is no service on the train itself.

Ninja Level

The elite warriors of the feudal age were known as the **ninja,** (忍者), and operated mainly in secret. With the knowledge gained at this level you'll be behaving almost like a real Japanese person.

Renting a karaoke box カラオケボックス

Karaoke (カラオケ), more or less translates as "empty orchestra" and owes its origins to musician and inventor *Daisuke Inoue* from Kōbe. In 1971 he began selling cassettes without the vocal track. It is one of Japanese people's favourite leisure activities.

Together with friends or colleagues you rent a **karaoke box,** (カラオケボックス), by the hour as a way of putting the stress of the office behind you with a beer and a sing-along. Two major chains with branches all over Japan, many of them close to railway stations, are called **Karaokekan** and **Big Echo.**

The **Utahiroba** chain is only to be found in and around Tokyo and is popular with school pupils and students because its low prices also include the "Softdrink Bar". Alongside soft drinks you can also help yourself to coffee, tea and soup. This means you not only save money, but also avoid potential communication problems when ordering.

Most of these establishments open at 11am and close again in the early hours at around 5am, when their Japanese customers make their way home with the first train of the day after a night spent drinking. Foreign tourists are seldom specifically catered for, and the websites are only in Japanese. But, don't worry, my tips will help you to throw yourself wholeheartedly into your karaoke adventure!

First of all, you need to register at reception. To do this, you enter your name on a piece of paper or on a list and say how long you would like to rent a box for. Sometimes you have to provide a telephone number or show your passport. For 30 minutes you pay between ¥80 and ¥800, depending on the location, time of day, day of the week and room.

Drinks are charged separately. There are also **"All-You-Can-Drink"** offers, *nomihōdai* (飲み放題), which include a choice of non-alcoholic or alcoholic drinks.

Occasionally, it is possible to choose the karaoke machine by the manufacturer. I recommend **Joysound** because the English menu is better, and many Japanese songs are included with subtitles written in the familiar Latin letters. You are then given a slip of paper showing the number of your allotted room and the time your booking ends. At Karaokekan there is also a rack with a selection of costumes to dress up in – this is really great fun. If you only want to give karaoke a try, I advise you go to **Karaokekan** or **Big Echo** during the daytime on a weekday, as you often only have to pay a quarter of the price charged after 7pm If you enjoyed it, you can plan your next visit for the evening. The best way to sing for as long as possible and as cheaply as possible is to choose a **"Free Time" offer** for the time between 11am and 7pm or 11pm and 5am; sometimes you only pay around ¥1500 and can stay for as long as you still have a voice!
www.gomap.de/**krke**

#Tip: Do you remember the scene in the film *Lost in Translation,* when *Bill Murray* sang karaoke with *Scarlett Johansson*? Sadly, room **601** at **Karaokekan** in **Shibuya** was closed in 2021. However, it is still possible to rent a room in the neighbouring building.
30–8 Udagawachō, Shibuya-ku, Tokyo, Tel.: 03-3462-0785

Singing karaoke カラオケ

Congratulations! You've made it as far as the karaoke box! The next step tells you how to operate the karaoke machine. First you have to change to the English menu. If you can't manage that, contact the staff via the telephone on the wall. Then choose the songs you want to sing, either by artist name or song title. Perhaps you should start off with something familiar? Search for **The Beatles** or **"Yesterday":** they are to be found on all systems. It usually takes a little while before the song starts. The machines used to run with a CD changer, but even the purely digital machines simulate a waiting time.

Time to get yourself ready, switch on the microphone until the music starts and the text appears on the screen. If there's a whistling sound due to feedback, you need to reduce the microphone volume. The dial is usually on the right at the bottom of the karaoke machine.

The most important dials are marked as follows:
Microphone volume: マイク(音量)
Music volume: ミュージック(音量)
Background music: **BGM (音量)**
Echo control: マイクエコー or エコーレベル

Using the "remote control" function, [リモコン], you can make further adjustments on the touchpad. The **Joysound** and **DAM** websites – in Japanese only – show the latest songs and where you can find the karaoke boxes with state-of-the-art equipment.
www.gomap.de/**kbox**

Don't make the same mistake as I did by only searching for your favourite songs. They are often not available or too difficult to sing. I've put together a list of ten English songs which are easy to sing and can be found on most machines as they are among the absolute favourite English-language hits in Japan.

Beatles: "Hey Jude", "Ob-la-di Ob-la-da", "Yesterday"
Bon Jovi: "It's My Life", "Livin' On A Prayer"
John Denver: "Take Me Home, Country Roads"
Lady Gaga: "Bad Romance", "Born This Way"
Taylor Swift: "Shake It Off", "We Are Never Ever Getting Back…"
For the more adventurous among you, why not try this schmaltzy Japanese classic "The Sukiyaki song", which has gained me extra points on numerous occasions in Japan!
Sakamoto Kyū [坂本九]: "Ue o muite arukō" [上を向いて歩こう]

Shortly before your authorised time is up, you are sometimes warned by a call on the wall telephone (which is normally also used for ordering drinks and food). At this point you say, *"Hai, wakarimashita",* "Yes, I understand", and hang up. If you leave punctually, you'll avoid having to pay for an extra 30 minutes.

#Tip: If you register on the Joysound website, install and log onto the **Joysound Karaoke Remote Control App,** where you can search for songs and artists and save them under "Favourites". In the karaoke box, you connect the machine with your smart phone ("pairing") and use it to select your songs directly and control the machine.

Budget feasting　　　　　　　　　　食べ物

To help you save money on **food,** *tabemono* (食べ物), I've already given you a few tips on teishoku (p. 48). Here are a few more for the more advanced Japan connoisseur:
Cheap restaurants need to save money on personnel and therefore have a ticket machine inside the entrance. This means you have to decide what you want to eat before you go in. Then you hand over the ticket to a member of staff and choose a table. Large chains sometimes have machines with a display and an English menu, but simple push-button versions are widespread. Sometimes there is a picture of the dish on the button, but normally these are only marked with Japanese characters. If you're lucky, you'll come across a sign with photos of the food and can compare the name or number underneath with the buttons on the machine. If you can't decipher anything, either ask the other diners in the queue behind you or a member of staff for help. I often ask for the restaurant's speciality or its most popular main course. This can generally be selected by pressing the **button at the top on the left.** You could also simply push this button and wait and see what you get.
A word of warning, though: in the rāmen restaurant **Tōshōmensō Karaya** in Akihabara the most popular dish is an extremely hot rāmen soup for ¥980! Thankfully, there is also a sign at the door to help you choose the right number (① very hot, ② hot) which you then press on the machine. If you like the sound of this hot soup, you'll find the restaurant via this link:
www.gomap.de/**krya**

Shortly before they close, **supermarkets** and **department stores** usually still have a lot of **food** which has to be eaten on the same day. Look out in particular for **bentō boxes** (p. 88), **onigiri, sushi, salads, sandwiches** and other ready meals. In order to sell these off quickly, prices are often reduced by half in the evening. You can recognise such goods easily by the additional, so-called **hangaku sticker,** [半額]. Sometimes the discount is also indicated using Arabic numbers. So if there is a supermarket, such as Kinokuniya or Seiyū or a konbini (p. 56) close to where you are staying, take a look in the evening and see if you can grab a bargain. You can heat up dishes such as omelettes, curry rice and noodles yourself in the shop's microwave oven, if you have no other possibility of doing so.

Don't confuse the characters for **best-before date** [賞味期限] and **use-by date** [消費期限] on fresh products with those for **processing date** [加工日], **manufacturing date** [製造日] or **delivery date** [納品日].

#Tip: The sophisticated bargain-hunter does not go to a normal supermarket in the evening, but visits the basement of a **luxury department store,** such as Mitsukoshi, Seibu, Takashimaya or Tōbu. The large gourmet food halls are called *depachika* (デパ地下), a word made up of department store, *depāto,* and basement, *chika.* Apparently some tourists are known to trawl through the food halls filling up on free tasting samples. For this reason, **foreigners,** *gaikokujin* (外国人), are only offered titbits at a few stands.

Shopping for souvenirs   おみやげ

It's never too early to start buying **souvenirs, *omiyage*** (おみやげ), when you are on holiday. I have already described Japanese traditions relating to souvenirs (p. 24). As the Japanese are insatiable travellers in their own country, you will find souvenir shops and typical local gifts in almost every tourist destination. **Paper lanterns, *chōchin*** (提灯), are to be had just about everywhere. They come in all colours and are decorated with the name of the sight or town in question. Since they are made of paper and plastic, they are light and, when folded in a box, take up hardly any room in your luggage. After a few years in Japan, the living room wall in my apartment was home to a sizeable collection of them. Back in Germany, however, instead of gathering dust, they were dispatched to a large box in the cellar. If you happen to have a basement party room, for example, such lanterns make the perfect decoration and give you the chance to entertain your guests with stories of the associated travel experiences.

Today, I prefer to buy high-quality souvenirs which I can use in the home, conjuring up memories of my travels while doing so. Many tourist spots boast fine **traditional arts and crafts** made of wood. In Kamakura, you'll find carved wooden items known as **Kamakura-bori** (鎌倉彫) which are characterised by their special lacquered finish. Hakone is renowned for **Yosegi-zaiku** (寄木細工), intricate marquetry work made of different types of wood. For years now, I've kept toothpicks in a small wooden box from Miyanoshita. These intricate mosaics also feature on picture frames, table mats, bowls, chopsticks and classic "puzzle boxes" with secret compartments.

Beautiful **ceramics** are to be had in all price categories, though many people are reluctant to buy large plates or tea cups because these could be damaged in transit. Smaller objects, such as little soy sauce bowls or chopstick racks, when packed carefully have survived all of my journeys home. When you make your purchase, ask staff to wrap any delicate items in bubble wrap, *puchi puchi,* to protect them on your return flight.

The hand-made **tea caddies** fashioned from sheet copper or cherry tree bark are real artworks. They keep forever, and the signs of wear give them a patina which makes them even more beautiful through years of use. No other country has such a wide selection of top-quality **brushes,** *tawashi* (束子), made of natural materials. Brushes for cleaning pots and pans, for example, are more expensive than disposable sponges, but they last far longer. Other type of souvenir which is characterised by varied design and innovative ideas is **stationery.** It is possible to buy such things as erasable ballpoint pens here in the West, but there is more choice in Japan. Presumably I don't need to mention cotton kimonos *(yukata),* chopsticks *(hashi),* consumer electronics, plastic sushi, damask steel knives, waving cats *(maneki-neko),* wooden dolls *(kokeshi)* and tea.
www.gomap.de/**svnr**

#Tip: Colourfully printed, rectangular cotton cloths called *tenugui* (手拭い) are ideal as handkerchiefs or towels when travelling. *Furoshiki* (風呂敷), on the other hand, are square and are great for wrapping presents (p. 118).

100 yen shops   100円ショップ

When it comes to buying souvenirs, it's worth mentioning the **100 Yen Shops,** *hyaku en shoppu* (100円ショップ). As the name suggests, most of their products cost a mere ¥100, plus ¥10 VAT. The most common chains in Japan are called **Daiso,** with over 2500 branches, and **Can Do** with around 1000. They are generally to be found in shopping centres and near railway stations.

The concept of these shops is so successful because a proportion of the goods are produced cheaply in China, and customers end up spontaneously buying other items not on their shopping lists. For this reason, you'll find everyday essentials in a 100 Yen Shop. These include all kinds of household goods, tableware, coffee filters, cling film and aluminium foil, office stationery, towels, coat hangers, clothes pegs, cleaning cloths, detergents, tools, sewing kits, toys, gardening products, clothes, home furnishings, brushes and bicycle accessories. They also sell food, especially confectionery and sweets, nibbles, snacks and drinks.

The Lawson chain not only runs the conventional konbinis with the blue logo, but also **Lawson Store 100,** this time with the logo in green. Here you can buy mainly food, household items and office stationery, all for ¥100 net. The most famous discounter, with 160 branches, is the **Don Quijote** chain, or **Donki** for short. They stock a similar range of goods to the 100 Yen Shops and most branches also offer convenient, 24-hour shopping. Popular items include sweets in various flavours such as Kitkat or Pocky, seaweed-flavoured potato crisps and instant rāmen.

There's also cosmetics, toiletries, Halloween costumes, cheap clothes and electronic goods. Branches are identified by the blue penguin wearing a crown. Goods are positioned at random throughout the stores so that shoppers find a host of other useless objects while searching for something specific.
The **Daiso** and **Miniso** chains now also have a handful of branches in America, Canada and Australia. Their biggest sellers are notebooks, cheap umbrellas, cutlery and chopstick sets, storage boxes, fluffy slippers, bathing shoes, anti-flu face masks and sleep masks.
www.gomap.de/**hysp**

#Tip: Just in case you don't stumble upon one of the above-named shops, here's a list of where to find the larger branches.
Tokyo: Daiso south of Harajuku station on Takeshita Dōri, **Donki Kabukichō** on Yasukuni Dōri and **Mega Donki Shibuya** less than 300 m from the famous road junction above Shibuya 109 department stores' on Bunkamura Dori.
Osaka: Daiso west of the castle in the Keihan City Mall, directly next to Exit 2 of Temmabashi station and **Donki Umeda** on Miya-kojima Dōri southeast of Umeda station or the **Donki Dotonbori** branch in the Ebisu Tower on the canal – you can't miss it thanks to the Ferris wheel.

50 shades of thanks　　　　ありがとう

What makes Japanese so difficult for Westerners to learn is not only that it is totally different to our languages and that it requires you to master three alphabets. The fact that the choice of words is dictated by the given situation and the relationship between speakers complicates matters further. That's why you won't find a long list of vocabulary in this book. Instead, I'd like to illustrate the complexity of the Japanese language, using the words "thank you" as an example.

"Sumimasen": You are sitting on a plane and accidentally spill some water on your fold-up table. Without you having to ask, the flight attendant brings you a serviette. You only use this as a word of thanks if you have caused someone some inconvenience. It is also simply used as a way of getting someone's attention, and you will hear it a lot in Japan.

"Dōmo": When your food is brought to you in a restaurant, you thank the service staff with *"dōmo"*. In an everyday business situation it is also widely used, but bear in mind that you should not say it to a superior. You can say *"dōmo"* to the intern, but never to your boss.

"Arigatō": This is used among friends and people of the same social status. If you receive a gift, it is better to use the superlative form **"dōmo arigatō"** for "thank you very much". Use both phrases when speaking to people you would address by their first name.

"Arigatō gozaimasu": Add the polite term *"gozaimasu"*, when addressing superiors, for example, your boss, teachers, police officers or parents-in-law. If the latter have just accepted your proposal of marriage to their daughter or son, you say **"dōmo arigatō gozaimasu"**. Politeness is important in Japan, so use *"gozaimasu"* when you address anyone who is of a higher social status or someone you would only address by their surname.

"Arigatō gozaimashita": If you wish to thank someone for something in the past, you must choose the correct tense. If you have enjoyed a few days at a small family-run guest house, *minshuku* (p. 46), you should say **"dōmo arigatō gozaimashita"** as you leave.

"Īe, kekkō desu": This means "no, thank you" if someone wants to pour you some more tea but you don't want any.

"Gochisō-sama deshita": This means "thank you for the delicious meal". Say this after a meal to which you have been invited or when leaving a restaurant to show how much you enjoyed the food.

"Otsukare-sama deshita": This is a charming way of saying goodbye to your colleagues after a long day at the office. Translated literally, it means "thank you for your efforts".

"Azāsu": This is slang, to be used among peers. As a man, only use it after the fourth beer with friends in a bar, *izakaya* (p. 112) or at karaoke (p. 90), if you are unable to express yourself otherwise. When using a messenger app with close friends, you may type **AZS.**

#Tip: Two pages are not enough, unfortunately, to demonstrate the intricacies of the Japanese language in relation to the words "thank you". Even if you take all this into account, I can't prevent you accidentally putting your foot in it by choosing the wrong word or phrase. If all else fails, you could still say **"thank you"** in English. Alternatively, in shops and restaurants, a friendly nod will often be sufficient, and is similarly favoured by many a tight-lipped Japanese.

Doing your washing 洗濯物

Sooner or later, anyone visiting Japan for a longer period will be confronted with the problem of having to do some **washing, *sentaku-mono*** (洗濯物).

The easiest option is of course to use the **hotel laundry service.** That's fine for the occasional blouse or shirt. Prices are reasonable, especially in modest **business hotels.** In an expensive luxury hotel, on the other hand, you have to pay more. Sometimes there is even an express service which returns your things the following day.

Konbinis often have a machine which lets you pop in your dirty shirt and collect it washed and ironed two days later from 9am. Admittedly, you have to register to use this service and be lucky enough to find a member of staff with the English skills to issue you with a customer card.

Dry-cleaners are cheaper than hotels. Many Japanese take their shirts there and collect them a few days later – freshly washed, starched and returned on a coat hanger or folded, as requested. When I lived in Japan, I made use of this cheap service. The only thing which bothered me was that I found the opening times inconvenient. The cleaners closest to my apartment was only open on certain days of the week at certain times. Since I started researching and writing travel guides, I've found myself almost always on the move until late in the evening and have given up using this practical but inflexible service.

Nowadays, I usually rent an apartment and make sure that it has a **washing machine** and a **tumble dryer**. Japanese washing machines are unsophisticated and only wash with cold water, but they do the job all the same. The spin cycle is also not as effective as in, say, a German washing machine, so you should allow more time for drying clothes. Ventilators in bathrooms often have a drying function, [乾燥], which you can use if you hang clothes up there.

Using a washing machine is really easy. You can buy ready-to-use sachets of washing powder which you scatter over the dirty washing. If necessary, turn on the tap above the machine and switch on [電源入]. Now press "Start", [スタート]; the rest of the programme runs automatically until the end of the spin cycle. Now and then you might have to set a specific programme, especially if you want your things to be dried after washing. Drying often takes between three and five hours.

#Tip: I'm actually opposed to the throw-away mentality, but if you need a new t-shirt or shirt quickly, you can buy them just about anywhere and they don't cost much. Sometimes prices are barely higher than for the hotel laundry service. The cheap label of the **Uniqlo** chain - in itself an inexpensive brand - is called **GU**.
www.gomap.de/**gujp**

At the launderette コインランドリー

Launderettes, or *"coin laundries"* (コインランドリー), are a cheap but more time-consuming way of doing your washing. Make sure you have collected enough ¥100 or even ¥50 coins, or use the change machines, as only these can be used to pay with. There are many different machines in use, but the procedure is always similar. First of all, clean the empty machine by pressing the button marked "Rinse drum" [ドラム洗浄] or "Drum Shower Button" [洗濯槽シャワーボタン] for at least ten seconds. This rinsing programme should be finished after a maximum of two minutes. You might have to insert your money before rinsing, so check the pictorial instructions either on the wall or inside the lid of the machine. Modern washing machines usually offer three options and display varying programme times and prices, depending on the amount of washing.

洗濯/乾燥	Wash and dry
洗濯のみ	Wash only
乾燥のみ	Dry

Press the appropriate button to choose the programme you want and insert the amount of money requested. Put the washing inside the drum and close the door.
Newer washing machines automatically add detergent. These are marked [洗剤は必要ありません].

Otherwise, add the detergent provided yourself. There are usually separate **tumble dryers** marked [乾燥機]. These are often powered by gas and cost ¥100 for 10 minutes. The washing can get very hot in these dryers and may shrink a little so never use them for delicate textiles.

Very simple machines, like the ones you often find in apartments, are top loaders. Put in the washing then add the detergent. The machines usually start automatically when you have inserted the money and closed the lid. Follow the same procedure for the tumble dryers. Some, however, have a start button, [スタート] which you have to press separately.

#Tip: If you are in Tokyo around Meguro, make sure you visit **Freddy Leck sein Waschsalon,** the launderette with a quirky German connection and excellent coffee. Over ten years ago, German actor, *Dirk Martens,* opened his own take on the launderette in the Moabit district or Berlin. Customers can now visit the branch in Tokyo, which opened in summer 2017. While you're waiting for your washing, you can enjoy German-style coffee and cake - a unique combination in Japan. The "Freddy Leck" range of laundry merchandise has been available in Japanese department stores for some years now.
www.gomap.de/**flsw**

Printing in konbinis　　　ネットプリント

Now it's time to have a go at using the network printers at **7-Eleven.** To do this, you need to register online at www.printing.ne.jp. This is currently only possible in Japanese. Fortunately, it is possible to register and navigate the website using a browser with an automatic translation function such as **Google Chrome.**

First of all, enter your e-mail address twice and click on the link in the e-mail sent to you. As is customary with this kind of service, you now need to agree to the terms and conditions of use. Don't worry, no costs are incurred until you actually print something in the store. When registering, you choose a user ID and a password and enter your name. You don't need to use a Japanese syllabary to write your name, just enter it phonetically using Latin letters, i.e. the way your name roughly sounds. (My name, **Axel,** sounds like **"akseru"** in Japanese.) When in doubt, just type anything. Then indicate how you found out about the service and click the button on the right (no newsletter). On the following page you confirm your entry with the blue button on the far right-hand side. You will now receive another e-mail in Japanese with your **login ID** and **date of registration.** That's all you need to do.

From now on, you just need to log into the website with your login ID and password and upload documents and photos (.docx .pdf .rtf .xlsx .pptx .xps .jpg .png .tif) to your account. Here you can also select the paper size (A4, A3, B4 or B5) and whether you want to print in colour or in black and white. If you wish you can also protect confidential documents with a 4-digit password.

Documents are stored for a maximum of one week. The maximum document size is 10 MB, and you have a maximum of 50 MB available storage. After a short time (press "Refresh") you will see an eight-character alphanumeric reservation number in the second column. If you haven't assigned a password, you only need this reservation number to print out your document in a 7-Eleven store. First, select the English menu on the multifunctional device in the konbini. Then press the [Print] button in the middle followed by the [netprint] button on the left. You should now quickly read through the "Cautionary Notes" and confirm by pressing [OK] at the bottom on the right. You will then be asked to enter your eight-digit reservation number and again confirm with [OK]. The next screen shows you a preview of the printed document and details of format, number of pages and printing costs. If everything is correct, press the dark blue button [Save & Next] (bottom right). To cancel, press [Reset & Back] (top right). Now all you need to do is indicate that you want to pay with coins (symbol, top right) and insert the right amount in the slot. Congratulations! You're almost there! Finish the job off by pressing the oval button marked [Start].

#Tip: The new **"Lite Version"** works without prior registration. Documents are only stored for one day, however. This version also works without the suggested apps. Simply press the orange button and proceed as above without logging in.
www.gomap.de/**ltpr**

Buying canned coffee 缶コーヒー

Drinks machines, *jidōhanbaiki* (自動販売機), can be found on every street corner in Japan. They sell a huge selection of drinks – alongside water, lemonade and tea, I particularly like the **canned coffee,** *kankōhī* (缶コーヒー), which you can get both warm or ice cold from brands such as Boss, DyDo, Georgia, Fire, Pokka, Nescafé, Roots, UCC and Wonda.

Before I was able to read kanji, buying a can of coffee was always a bit of a lottery; I usually got bitter, black coffee or coffee with milk, when what I really wanted was coffee *with* sugar and *no* milk. To make sure the same thing doesn't happen to you, I've put together a list of key designations:

1. Any kind, as long as it's coffee (2-6):
    コーヒー or [picture with coffee beans]
2. Black coffee, no sugar, often in black can:
    Black, ブラック, **0 kcal** or 無糖 (no sugar)
3. Black coffee, a little sugar, no milk:
    微糖 (a little sugar) or 甘さ (lightly sweetened)
4. Coffee with milk and sugar:
    微糖 (a little sugar) or 甘さ (lightly sweetened) *and*
    牛乳100% (100% cow's milk) or ミルク (milk)
5. Coffee with lots of milk, often no sugar
    Latte or ラテ
6. Coffee with lots of milk, often with sugar
    Café au Lait or カフェオレ

#Tip: This list works for 80% of all cans, but if it doesn't help with one machine, just try the next one.

Shogun Level

The **shogun** (将軍) ranks higher than all samurai and ninja. Now that you have successfully mastered all previous levels, you can devote yourself to the final ten steps and learn about the religion, culture and character of the Japanese.

Shrines and temples 神社/お寺

The majority of Japanese people are followers of Shintoism and Buddhism, which is why you will find **shrines,** *jinja* (神社), and **temples,** *o-tera* (お寺), everywhere but only a handful of Christian churches. The single most distinctive feature of a shrine is its **main gate,** *torii* (鳥居), through which you enter the sacred inner shrine area. These torii are usually made of wood and painted red, although some are unpainted and others made of stone. Do not walk through the centre of the torii – this path is reserved for the gods – instead, keep to the right or left. The devout bow briefly before the torii and remove any headwear. A little further on to one side, there is a **water-filled basin,** *temi-zuya* (手水屋), for rinsing the hands and mouth. Using a ladle, you take some water and wash your left and right hand, then rinse the mouth by drinking from the left hand. After washing the left hand once again, you wash the ladle and put it back. If you are unsure of yourself, watch how the other visitors behave or read the signs, if any. Once you have reached the **main shrine,** you bow briefly and ring the bell – if there is one – to inform the gods of your visit. Now it is time to make a donation, which you usually put into a large wooden offertory box. It's up to you to decide how much you would like to give, but if you happen to have a coin with a hole in it (¥5 or ¥50), use that. Next, take two deep bows and then clap your hands twice before putting your hands together to pray. After praying in silence for a moment, take a deep bow once again. If you want to be on the safe side, express your wish or thanks to the gods in written form. To do this, buy a **wooden plaque,** *ema* (絵馬), for ¥500 and write your message on it with a felt-tip pen and hang it up on the rack or tree nearby.

If you'd prefer to hide your wish from prying eyes, you can also write a letter to the gods, enclosing a donation!

So-called **"paper fortunes"**, *o-mikuji* (おみくじ), which you can buy for ¥100-400, are also very popular. To get one, you shake a wooden box and pull out a stick with a number. Say the number at the booth marked みくじ and you are given your piece of paper. At larger shrines it is often possible to get one written in English. If you are not satisfied with the result or simply not sure of whether it means something good or bad, just fold it up and tie it to the tree or rack again.

When visiting temples, the same rules apply with regard to purification and prayer rituals except you do not clap your hands. There is usually also an incense burner where people, believing in its healing power, can waft incense over the affected areas of their body.

#Tip: Buy yourself a **talisman,** *o-mamori* (お守り), to bring you good luck in all kinds of circumstances: health, happiness, love, marriage, driving or exams. They are offered for between ¥700 and ¥1200. The *"IT o-mamori"*, available at the **EDOCCO** on the site of the **Kanda-Myōjin Shrine** in Tokyo, is an interesting choice and costs ¥1000. It takes the form of two green stickers and a plaque the size of a credit card which you stick to your computer or carry around in your purse or wallet in order to protect against computer crashes, viruses and hardware defects. The talisman has worked extremely reliably on my computer for years now.

www.gomap.de/**kdmy**

Getting drunk in an izakaya 居酒屋

The Japanese like going out for a drink with their colleagues after work, a practice known as **"nomunication"** - derived from the word **"nomu"** which means "to drink" and **"communication"**. During my time in Japan I enjoyed these evenings a lot, as the collegial atmosphere in the department was boosted by the chance to communicate more openly outside the office. Such evenings often begin in a **Japanese bar,** *izakaya* (居酒屋), which in addition to a large drinks menu also offer a wide selection of food.

Instead of each person ordering food for themselves, the chosen dishes are placed in the centre of the table and everyone helps themselves to small portions. The advantage here is that you get to try out a huge range of different dishes. The most popular include soya beans, *edamame* (枝豆), pizza (ピザ), radish salad, aubergines, sashimi, mackerel and **grilled chicken kebabs,** *yakitori* (焼き鳥).

As far as drinks are concerned, you start off with **beer,** *bīru* (ビール), but don't start drinking until everyone has raised their glass in a toast. Then you move on to **sake,** *nihonshu* (日本酒), **wine** or **whisky.** Each person is given the appropriate glass, and it is customary to pour each other's drinks, taking care to hold bottle and glass respectively with both hands. Where possible, you should not pour your own drinks. The fact that the glasses are small helps to minimize the risk of getting too drunk. I had very attentive colleagues, however, who were keen to get me drunk. Again and again, they would tell me to drink up so that they could give me a refill! Late in the evening, however, they were content to let me just sip from my glass before refilling.

There is also a wide range of high-proof Japanese liquor such as **rice schnapps**, *awamori* (泡盛), from Okinawa and **shōchū** (焼酎), which is distilled from just about anything. Shōchū is commonly mixed with soft drinks to make a **highball** or **chūhai**. If you indulge in too many highballs, you are guaranteed a hangover the following morning, particularly if cheap shōchū is used. At the end, either the boss pays the bill, or it is split by the number of people present. It is not customary for guests to receive a separate bill in Japan. When out with friends, too, the amount is divided up equally, and you put your share on the table in cash. Those who have either had enough alcohol, a long journey home or an important appointment the following morning leave at this point after the first stage. A smaller group often moves on to another bar or for a karaoke session (p. 90), to conduct a little more nomunication! If you miss the last train around midnight, you can carry on partying until the early hours, in which case further changes of venue are common.

#Tip: An evening in a Japanese bar is not as expensive as you might think and should definitely feature in your holiday in Japan. There are a number of cheap chains which charge roughly ¥3000 per person and leave their guests feeling well fed and slightly tipsy after approximately two hours. English menus are rare, but most have plenty of photos, or you can order directly via a tablet which with any luck can be switched to English.
www.gomap.de/**izky**

Surviving the forces of nature   地震/台風

Having lived in Japan for some time, I was no longer taken by surprise by **earthquakes, *jishin*** (地震), and took them in my stride in the same way as I did with the regular **typhoons, *taifū*** (台風). I experienced my first severe earthquake as a student during my internship semester at a Japanese company in Saitama, northwest of Tokyo. I got the shock of my life when, standing on the third floor of an ordinary factory building, everything began to shake. The shelves were swaying to such an extent that I sought refuge under a laboratory workbench. This caused much amusement among my Japanese colleagues, who calmly carried on working as if nothing had happened – just a harmless earthquake, briefly referred to in the evening news.

The tragedy in Fukushima on 11 March 2011 finally showed the rest of the world that there are not only harmless earthquakes in Japan. Here are a few tips on how to react:

If you are inside a building at the time of the quake, you should not leave in a panic, but seek shelter under a sturdy table or door frame and hold on tight. You should also protect your head, for example, with a cushion. Under no circumstances should you use the lift. In public buildings, hotels, restaurants and department stores, you should follow the staff's instructions.

If you are already outdoors, make for an open space as quickly as possible. Keep as far away as you can from houses, street lights, trees and overhead power lines and poles to avoid being injured by broken glass and other falling debris. If you are near the coast, run inland to higher ground. You should only return when the official **tsunami** all-clear is given.

Tidal waves can occur long after the actual earthquake, and further subsequent waves are possible. Information is flashed onto all TV screens across all channels. Switch on NHK and activate **English** using the button [音声切替]. Information is also available on the website of the Japan Meteorological Agency **JMA** or by **push notification** from the "**NHK World-Japan**" app (p. 28). Alternatively, information is broadcast in several languages on radio frequency 76.1 MHz in the event of a catastrophe. The **emergency number** for ambulance and fire brigade is **119,** for the police **110.**

Alongside earthquakes and tsunamis, there are frequent typhoons between August and October which mainly affect southern Japan but can also bring heavy rainfall and violent storms to Tokyo. Thankfully, weather reports warn of typhoons several days in advance, giving details of when and where they are likely to hit the Japanese mainland. When such storms reach their peak, you should avoid being outdoors if you can. You'll find some suggestions for indoor activities on the following page. In hotels and other solid buildings you will be safe from typhoons. Things can get a little unpleasant if you happen to be in a simple Japanese wooden house, as these can get thoroughly shaken by such a storm. Close doors, windows and shutters beforehand.
www.gomap.de/**fona**

#Tip: After a typhoon has passed over Tokyo, I recommend going to one of the city's observation decks. With any luck, you will experience the only summer day when it is possible to get a good view of Fuji-san from Tokyo. The strong winds make for clear air and fabulous views.

Beating the rain 雨

The **teru teru bōzu** is an old Japanese tradition, aimed at bringing on fine weather. Small dolls are made out of white paper or fabric and hung under the eaves of buildings. Care must be taken, though: if the doll is hung upside down, it will rain. The **ame ame bōzu** custom is widely followed by farmers who are hoping for **rain,** *ame* (雨), to fall on their dry fields. If their wish is fulfilled, the doll is drenched in sake as a reward. The weather god is not always appeased by this tradition. If you're travelling between June and September in particular, there's no escaping the odd rainy day.

You can easily cope with a little light drizzle, but you should take care not to be caught outside at the wrong time if there is a **typhoon** approaching. It is also possible that overland railway services are halted at such times. Luckily, I have been spared this up to now, but some of my Japanese colleagues have had to spend whole nights standing on overcrowded suburban trains on their way home from work when they ground to a halt due to bad weather. If the weather forecast says the typhoon is still some distance away, you can of course stay outside, but don't use an umbrella. A high-quality, breathable **waterproof jacket** with a hood comes in handy here. In cities during the **rainy season,** keep your travel plans flexible and be prepared for a few rainy days. Thanks to the superb infrastructure, there's plenty to see and do at such times. Why not visit a **museum** or art **exhibition?**

In **Tokyo,** buy a **day ticket** (p. 51) for the subway and try this experiment on the Ginza Line: how far can you get without having to put up your umbrella? You could spend an entire day **shopping** between Shimbashi station (G08) and Mitsukoshi station (G12), as the extensive underground network of the individual stations takes you directly to the department stores.

What's more, there are also many **covered shopping streets,** e.g. Shin-Nakamise Dōri in Asakusa (G19). On the Chūō Line, to the west of Shinjuku at Kōenji station there is one such street: the "Kōenji Pal Shopping Arcade" begins directly to the south-west of the station. From Meguro, take the Meguro Line to Musashi-Koyama station. To the south of here you'll find both a short and a long covered shopping street. The very large **shopping centre,** known as Solamachi, is located right under the Tokyo Skytree and is ideal for souvenir shopping. And you can get there from Oshiage station without getting your feet wet. Are you not interested in shopping? Would you prefer to do something more active? Then why not go for a **karaoke session** (p. 90), visit a **video games centre** or squander your money on the slot machines in an **amusement arcade,** *pachinko* (パチンコ)?
www.gomap.de/**rain**

#Tip: Other cities also offer plenty of opportunities for some rainy day shopping. In **Kyoto** there are the covered shopping streets, Shijō, Nishiki and Teramachi. The Shinsaibashi shopping centre in **Osaka** runs from Umeda as far as Namba, covering an overall distance of two kilometres.

Wrapping presents 風呂敷

Traditionally in the Edo period (1603–1868) goods were packed for transport and clothes carried around in the bathhouse in a **square cloth, *furoshiki*** (風呂敷). In contrast to the rectangular **tenugui** (30 × 90 cm) which is made of cotton, a furoshiki can also be made of silk or today even of synthetic fibres. Depending on its intended use, its sides measure between 45 and 100 cm, but larger cloths are used for transporting boxes.

The invention of the plastic bag led to a drastic reduction in the use of the furoshiki, but the tradition is now being revived for reasons of environmental protection. Today, people like to use them for packing bentō boxes (p. 88), wrapping presents, or as a bag to carry things in. The practical aspect of transporting your lunch box in a square cloth is that it doubles as a "blanket" for your picnic in the park or lunch on the Shinkansen.

When giving Japanese confectionery as a gift, I like to use furoshiki measuring around 50 × 50 cm, which lets me wrap any rectangular object of a good 20 cm in length. As a rule of thumb, the diagonal of the cloth should be approximately three times the length of the present. Place the object in the centre of the cloth along a diagonal and then take one corner and fold it over the object, tucking it underneath. Then take the opposite corner and lay it across the object, keeping it as smooth as possible. Bring the remaining fabric ends together and tie them in a single or double knot on top of the present. If you use fabric with a simple pattern and are not particularly concerned about getting a perfect knot, that's all there is to it.

The correct Japanese method of wrapping gifts for special occasions is, of course, a lot more complicated. The various folding techniques and knots each have a special meaning. On very formal occasions, for example, the knot is concealed by a corner of the fabric. If the gift marks a more serious matter, no knots are used at all. Instead, the cloth is simply folded around it and the end tucked in rather like an envelope. Gifts of money are wrapped in a small furoshiki made of silk. The colour chosen depends on whether the present is for a wedding or a funeral. As long as you're only wrapping a few souvenirs for back home, you don't need to worry about such details.

If you can't wait to find out more about the different furoshiki folding techniques, there are a number of English-language books available giving illustrated instructions. My favourite is *The Furoshiki - A Comprehensive Guide,* published by the Japan Furoshiki Association. I bought my copy of the 48-page guide for ¥302 at the tourist information office in the basement of the Kyōbashi Edogrand (Exit 1, Kyōbashi station) in Tokyo. You can also buy it at the Tokyo National Museum shop in Ueno Park. Unfortunately, it is not widely available outside Japan, though you could try your luck on an online auction platform.
www.gomap.de/**frsh**

#Tip: Choose furoshiki with individual designs and colours for wrapping souvenirs for your family and friends. This valuable gift wrap also gives presents from Japan an authentic feel.

Going to a love hotel　　　ラブホテル

In certain districts of Tokyo, such as on the hill in Dōgenzaka in **Shibuya,** Kabukichō in **Shinjuku** or **Uguisudani** near the station, you will notice a host of hotels with lavishly decorated façades. Some have names such as St Moritz, Villa Giulia or Hotel Stellato. These unmistakable so-called **love hotels** are distinguished by their signs indicating prices for short visits, **"Rest"** and overnight stays, **"Stay".** Instead of love hotel, you also find designations such as **amuse, couple** or **fashion hotels.** In contrast to the otherwise small Japanese hotel rooms, the rooms in such establishments are often generously proportioned. At the more up-market love hotels, standard features include **flat-screen TVs** and a selection of films plus huge **whirlpool baths.** Western-style interiors are popular in love hotels, presumably because they bring back fond honeymoon memories for many Japanese couples. Apart from Hawaii, Europe and Bali are also popular destinations with honeymooners, and hotels are furnished accordingly. Love hotels are, in fact, mostly used by married couples, who often suffer from a lack of privacy in their own home. It is also possible for any couple to book a room without having to present a marriage certificate. Consequently, fathers are known to become slightly nervous the first time their daughter goes shopping with her boyfriend to Shibuya! **Discretion** is taken extremely seriously in love hotels. When checking in, couples first choose an available room. Sometimes there are pictures of rooms currently on offer. Payment is either via an impersonal machine or at a counter, where only the hands of the person behind it are visible through a small gap.

Guests arriving by car can have its registration plates covered up as a special service. This is particularly important in rural areas, as nothing could be more embarrassing for a Japanese couple than their car being spotted in the car park by their neighbours. That's probably one reason why people choose cars in inconspicuous, standard colours.

Tariff systems in love hotels vary greatly, but **prices** for a stay of two or three hours start at around ¥3000. An overnight stay will cost at least two or three times that amount. **#Note:** As soon as guests have left the room, it is generally not possible to return. Around 15 minutes before the allotted time runs out, there may be a phone call to the room to remind guests to check out punctually. In response, the guest says, *"Hai, wakarimashita"* and hangs up. Guests who miss this deadline have to pay extra.

Some hotels are trying to shake off their vaguely sleazy image by offering accommodation to tourists via international booking portals. Prices are similar to those of business hotels, but bear in mind that you should anticipate audible nocturnal activity in neighbouring rooms!

#Tip: If you are perhaps travelling with your partner on a budget and therefore staying in a capsule hotel or youth hostel, you might like to book a room at a cheap love hotel for an hour or two. Avoid weekends and the early evening, however. Prices are sometimes lower after 10pm. On the **Couples** website you can view pictures of the rooms before booking.

www.gomap.de/**lvht**

Finding yourself 座禅/武道/茶道

If you take a closer look at Buddhism in Japan, you will quickly come across **Zen Buddhism,** made familiar in the West by the practice of **sitting meditation** known as *zazen* (座禅). My first contact was years ago with the **Sōtō school,** which places particular emphasis on meditation and is the largest Zen Buddhism community in Japan.

In order to get to know zazen, I visited the **Chōkokuji Temple** in Roppongi one Monday evening. Initial instructions and subsequent training were in Japanese, and there was only a flyer in English, published by the head Zen temple, **Eiheiji,** in Fukui Prefecture. As this is a strict Buddhist temple, I chose to wear a pair of dark grey trousers, black socks and a plain blue t-shirt for my visit. However, at the end of training, I was still asked to wear slightly more subdued colours next time. My shirt was probably too pale, so make sure you only wear dark grey or black. If you'd prefer a less strict temple, where you can participate without knowing any Japanese and don't have to register in advance, you should go to the **Engaku-ji Temple** in Kamakura. Every Saturday, except in August, there are introductory events in the Kojirin building starting at 1pm The temple is located close to Kita-Kamakura station. The dress code is not quite as strict here as at Chōkokuji; they even recommend wearing a track suit. Generally speaking, you should not wear tight clothing when practising zazen meditation. Shorts in summer and thick jumpers in winter are both inappropriate. Belts, ties and wristwatches should be removed before meditating. I won't give a detailed description of procedure here; I suggest you visit an introductory event instead.

If zazen is not your cup of tea, Japanese culture offers you a number of other ways of "finding yourself".

If you're a sporty type, go **"the way of the warrior"**, *budō* (武道). The modern Japanese **martial arts** disciplines, such as aikidō, iaidō, jōdō, jūdō or kendō have one thing in common: their main objective is not to defeat others, but to overcome yourself through continuous training and striving for perfection. This philosophy is based on Zen Buddhism and the virtues of the **samurai**. The old, traditional samurai martial arts are known as **koryū-bujutsu** and have been handed down unchanged to successive generations. Here in the West, there are also training centres, *dōjō,* where these are taught. The **school,** *ryūha*, of Hokushin Ittō-Ryū Hyōhō is taught at the Chiba-Dōjō. What's special about this school is that it is no longer based in Japan. It has been operating in Munich since 2016 under the direction of *Ōtsuka Ryūnosuke Masatomo*. German by birth, the 7th sōke adopted a Japanese name while a pupil and protégé of the 6th sōke, *Ōtsuka Yōichirō Masanori*.

Created by *Sen no Rikyū* (1522-91), the ritualised **"way of tea" ceremony,** *sadō* (茶道), is also practised to this day according to the sōke system at the Mushakōjisenke, Omotesenke and Urasenke schools founded by his three great grandsons. If you get the chance on your travels to participate in a tea ceremony you should take it.

www.gomap.de/**zbds**

#Tip: There are regular demonstrations of the way of tea according to the **Ueda Sōko** and **Urasenke** schools in many Western cities. Take part in one in preparation for your trip to Japan.

Searching for ikigai 生き甲斐

A new trend known as **ikigai** is permeating Western bestseller lists, promising to reveal the secret of Japanese longevity. The quest to find one's ikigai is all about finding your **passion.** In the West, the same idea is described as one's **calling** or a sense of **self-fulfilment.** The word ikigai brings together the words for life, *iki,* and value, *kai,* and can be translated as **"meaning of life"** or, more freely, as "something to get up for in the morning". Ideally, this ikigai is an activity which not only gives you pleasure, but which you are good at, serves the common good and, if possible, earns enough money for you to live on in the process. Once you've found your ikigai, a zest for life and a feeling of satisfaction will set in which ultimately are the key to living to a great age, while at the same time staying physically and mentally fit.

Dr Shigeaki Hinohara is a prime example; he was a practising physician until a few months before his death. He was convinced that life was about making a contribution to society. His desire to help others was the factor which drove him to get up early every morning. Drawing up a calendar for five years at a time, he would set himself long-term goals and was determined, for example, to live to see the Olympic Games in 2020. In July, 2017 he passed away at the age of 105.

Very few typical Japanese office workers, *salarymen,* are likely to be pursuing their calling, but are probably just doing their job primarily as a way of earning a living. The ikigai can even be restricted entirely to your private life and serve to compensate for the stress of office work and its many overtime hours.

It could be a hobby, for example, going hiking in the mountains every weekend, practising one of the martial arts or playing a musical instrument, being an avid, ambitious photographer, doing flower arranging (ikebana), growing bonsai, or painting pictures. Equally, it could also be expressed as your personal commitment to your family or voluntary work for other people.

One of the main lessons learned from ikigai is not to expect too much. You don't necessarily have to turn your life upside down or quit your job, in order to pursue your supposed dream. It's often enough just to concentrate on your daily tasks and perform them conscientiously and without haste. Take pleasure in the little things in life, help others and be grateful when others help you. In general, the Japanese interact in a greater spirit of harmony than we do in the West. This has a positive effect on employee motivation and team spirit, leading to a greater sense of fulfilment than in Western workplaces.

#Tip: In the now sheer number of books on Ikigai, there is unfortunately also a lot of trash literature that is not worth the paper it is printed on. Actually, there is only one book in the plethora of publications that I can recommend to you in good conscience, namely **"The Little Book of Ikigai: The secret Japanese way to live a happy and long life"** written by neuroscientist *Ken Mogi*. It was published in 2018 by Quercus Editions Ltd. in London.

Internalising Ichi-go Ichi-e　　　一期一会

For me personally, the insights gained from the philosophy of **Ichi-go Ichi-e** marked a pivotal moment in my reflections on the Japanese way of life. But it took many years to reach this point. To spare you this long journey, I will report on my experiences and give you some background information on this **philosophy.** I first heard the term ichi-go ichi-e at a **tea tasting.** I was part of a small group that had come together to prepare and try some exquisite Japanese teas. We ended up having an extremely enjoyable discussion about our experiences of tea and Japan. I learned a lot about tea, its cultivation and how it is served and drunk in Japan. The female **tea master** was just as intrigued to hear about my previous experiences, so what began as a conventional talk was transformed into a stimulating conversation between the participants. Time flew by and, before I knew it, two hours had passed although the event was only scheduled to last for one. At the end, the tea master said that the shared tea drinking experience had been a beautiful example of ichi-go ichi-e. In fact, the concept originated in the tea ceremony and is attributed to tea master *Sen no Rikyū* (p. 123). Ichi-go Ichi-e literally means "one moment, one meeting", but actually signifies something like **a once-in-a-lifetime encounter.**

The second time I came across it was at a high-class kaiseki restaurant in Berlin which has adopted ichi-go ichi-e as its philosophy. As with a Japanese tea ceremony, much thought and effort had gone into the design of the restaurant interior as well as the choice and preparation of the exquisite food.

A sense of mutual respect and heartfelt interaction in a cosy setting guarantees that both guest and host feel at ease. The chef prepared each course in front of the guests and personally handed the food to them across the counter. As a consequence, the customary "barrier" between chef and guest, resulting from their spatial separation and the presence of service personnel, was lost. I forgot all my worries and concentrated solely on the unique atmosphere and enjoying the meal.

#Tip: Take the following basic principles to heart and from now on enjoy every moment in the here and now. Value each encounter as something truly unique in life; after all, many of them will never be repeated. Even if you meet the same group of people for the same reason and in the same place at some point in the future, it is impossible to recapture the atmosphere of the initial encounter. Each interaction during your trip to Japan is a unique moment in your life – enjoy it!

Ordering a personal seal   判子

Congratulations! You are now almost Japanese! All you need now is your own **personal seal,** *hanko* (判子). Among Japanese, it is not your signature that counts but a registered wooden seal which you use, for example, for contracts, forms and bank transfers. During my time in Japan I didn't have one and had to always squeeze my signature on a bank transfer form into the tiny circle intended for the seal. This caused trouble, as it was often not identical to the signature I provided when I opened my account. I used a simple surname seal made of rubber at work for officially releasing data sheet translations. I suggest having a personal seal made to remind you of your trip to Japan.

#Tip: In **Yanaka Ginza** in Tokyo there is a small shop called **Shinimonogurui** where you can have a rubber seal with your name and a funny picture on it made for ¥2600. The staff do not speak English but they can help you to fill in the order form.
Select picture, font and colour by pointing to the wall. To translate your first or surname – there won't be room for both – into the phonetic syllabary katakana, write the name in capital letters on the piece of paper and say it out loud a few times until the lady behind the counter is satisfied. You can collect your seal after around 30 minutes.
www.gomap.de/**hnko**

End - 終わり

Index

24-hour stores 30, 56
100 Yen Shops 98
Adapters 19
Addresses 53
Air conditioners 54
Airport Limousine Bus 86
Alcohol 112
All-You-Can-Drink 91
Animal cafés 43
Apple Maps 16, 53
Apple Pay 27
Area maps 52
Arts and crafts 96
ATMs 23, 57
Autumn foliage 11
Avoiding waste 59
Awamori (schnapps) 113
Bargains 94
Bars 112
Bathhouses 78
Beer 112
Bentō boxes 88, 95
Blowing your nose 75
Booking portals 12
Bowing 74
Breakfast 30
Buddhism 110, 122
Business cards 75
Buying clothes 103
Café chains 31
Car rental 72

Cash 23, 57
Cat cafés 42
Ceramics 97
Cherry blossom season 10
Chopsticks 32
Cigarette machines 61
City maps 52
Cleaning clothes 102, 104
Coffee 31, 56, 108
Confectionery 25, 44, 56
Conveyor-belt sushi 40
Day ticket (bus) 85
Direct flights 13
Doing your washing 102
Doors 82
Drinks machines 108
Earthquakes 114
Eating on a budget 94
Emergency number 115
Entrance tickets 57
Escalators 75
Evening meal 48
Finding your passion 124
Flight bookings 12
Furoshiki (cloth) 97, 118
Futon (mattress) 46
Gestures 80
Golden Week 11
Google Earth 17
Google Maps 16, 53
Goshuin-chō 70

Green tea 62
Greeting 74
Guest houses (minshuku) 46
Hakone 46
Hand gestures 81
Hotel bookings 12
Ichi-go Ichi-e 126
Ikigai (passion) 124
Internet 20
Izakaya (Japanese bar) 112
Japanese numbers 47
Japan Rail Pass 14
Japan Transit Planner 18
Kaiseki (multi-course meal) 46
Kaiten-zushi 40
Karaoke 90, 92
Kōban (police) 53
Konbinis 30, 56
Kyoto 43, 45, 117
Launderettes 104
Left luggage 86
Lockers 86
Love hotels 120
Luggage forwarding service 87
Lunch boxes 88, 95
Luxury department stores 95
Map apps 16
Martial arts 123
Matcha tea 44
Meditation 122
Mineral springs 78
Miso soup 30, 41, 48
Mobile phone/cellphone 20

Nagoya 37, 43
Network printers 106
NHK World-Japan 28, 115
Nikko 88
Non-smokers 60
Noodle soups 38
Obon (public holiday) 11
Oden (stew) 56
Offline maps 17
Omiyage (small gifts) 24
Onigiri (rice balls) 56, 95
Onsen (hot springs) 46, 78
OpenStreetMap 17
Osaka 39, 43, 99, 117
Packing 22
Paper fortunes 111
Paper lanterns 96
PASMO/Suica 26, 50
Personal fulfilment 124
Philosophy of life 126
Photocopiers 57
Pitfalls 74
Planning your trip 10
Pork cutlet 36
Praying 110
Prepaid SIM, eSIM 21
Presents 24, 118
Queuing 62, 74
Rainy season 10, 116
Rāmen noodles 38
Reading menus 47
Rental cars 72
Rental SIM 20

Restaurants 18, 28, 94
Roaming 20
Rules of behaviour 74
Ryokan (inn) 46
Sake 25, 112
Saying goodbye 74
Saying thank you 100
Seasons 10
Selfie sticks 76
Sentō (bathhouses) 78
Service concept 62
Shinkansen 14
Shintoism 110
Shōchū (schnapps) 113
Shoes 68
Shopping centres 117
Shrines 110
Sliding doors 82
Small gifts 24, 96
Smartphones 18
Smokers 60
Soba noodles 38
Sockets 19
Souvenirs 25, 96, 98
Spring 10
Stamps/name seals 71, 128
Stationery 97
Subway 50
Suitcases 86
Supermarkets 95
Sushi etiquette 34
Taking photographs 76
Taking the bus 84

Talisman 111
Tatami mats 46
Tattoos 79
Taxis 63, 64
Tea caddies 97
Tea ceremonies 44, 123
Teishoku (Japanese menus) 48
Temples 110
Tenugui (cotton cloths) 97
The meaning of life 124
Thermal spas 46, 78
Tickets 26
Tipping 65
Toilets 66, 83
Tokyo 39, 43, 99, 117
Tokyo Subway Ticket 51
Tonkatsu (cutlet) 36
Translations 19
Tsunami 115
Tumble dryers 105
Typhoons 114, 116
Udon noodles 38
Visit Japan Web 132
Wagashi (confectionery) 44
Wasabi (horseradish) 34, 40
Washing machines 103
Waste disposal 58
Waterproof jacket 22, 116
Wheelchairs 28
Wi-fi 20, 56
Wi-fi routers 21
Yakitori (chicken skewers) 112
Zazen (sitting meditation) 122

Notes

To help you correctly pronounce unfamiliar words, I use the kunrei transcription system, as learned by Japanese schoolchildren. Long vowels are indicated by a macron (¯) above the letter. If you still have difficulty making yourself understood, point to the printed character at the same time.

Prices are correct as of June 2024 and include 10% VAT. The information and tips contained in this book have been compiled in good faith and carefully cross-checked. Nevertheless, I accept no liability for erroneous content.

By using **short links,** written as follows "www.gomap.de/**xxxx**" I can ensure that printed internet addresses do not become obsolete and provide you with the latest information and additional updates. To save you having to type a lot, add "www.gomap.de" to the favourites list on your computer or mobile phone. Then you only need to type in the four lower-case letters in bold, for example, "books" for an overview of my **books** or "upda" for the **latest updates** and a list of my **social media channels** and **blogs.** For detailed information on the latest entry procedures using **Visit Japan Web,** please see "www.gomap.de/**co19**".

★★★★★ Have you enjoyed this book?

It would help me a lot if you leave a rating or short review on Amazon. Many thanks! I also look forward to hearing your comments by e-mail: japan@axelschwab.com
www.gomap.de/**fes**

Printed in Great Britain
by Amazon